DEDICATION

This book is dedicated to Tina, Olivia and Eva

CONTENTS

ACKNOWLEDGMENTS

From an early age I discovered the fascinating world of acknowledgments, since here was a way of getting closer to the writer and the artist. As I became an avid reader, my interest in acknowledgements grew, especially when I realized how difficult it is write a book of your own. There is something extremely difficult, even impossible, about naming everyone who has contributed to your work and to your personal development when you have been influenced by so many people, without at time even noticing their contribution or knowing they would have such a substantial impact.

I want to start by apologizing to anyone I may have omitted, I did not do so willingly or knowingly. There are some in particular who have given me license over the years to operate freely within their businesses in a way that has directly enriched this text.

My thanks and gratitude go out to you all.

Introduction

The Coaching Secret – The Ugly Truth, is the follow up to the Leadership Secret – The Ugly Truth. The leadership secret was a record of my leadership journey, which focused on coaching as a style of leadership. In the leadership secret, there is a chapter dedicated to coaching, but not from a technical perspective.

As a result of the success of the leadership secret, and feedback suggesting that I produce a more technical book, focusing on coaching, the coaching secret explores coaching and reveals the secrets to coaching that are invaluable to success.

This book will be a valuable guide to those who coach, irrespective of your level of experience. Coaching centres on the occupation of coaching traditionally, however, coaching is employed in leadership, management, mentoring, counselling, parenting and teaching to name but a few. The coaching relationship is the key through which individual, group and organisations are able to make and sustain change.

For those that are new to coaching, the coaching secret, will provide an insight into how you can build your confidence and expertise to coach. It explores how you may answer some of the essential questions that are likely to be asked. It will help you to understand more deeply, and encourage your development as a coach.

To the experienced coach, this book will build on and examine aspects of coaching and the secrets to becoming an truly exceptional coach. Through examples taken from my own practice and those that I have worked with, we will explore how to discover those essential instruments that facilitate successful coaching.

It is interesting to find that most of the coaching literature presents only a partial view of coaching. This is the same of individuals who instruct individuals on the how to coach. But what about the "what" and the "what if". What does practical coaching look like? How many times have you read a book, or taken part in a training event that was all about the author or trainers success.

Contrary to some appealing claims of other books, there are no quick wins in business, and great coaching is a skill, that requires a depth of understanding. It requires practice if it is to release potential. Reading this book will not develop you into an expert coach, but it will help you to recognise the value and enormous potential that coaching has. It will set you on a journey of self-awareness, that will have a profound on your success, both in the workplace and home.

As with any new skill, adopting a coaching methodology requires commitment, practice and time before it comes second nature. Some who read this will find that coaching comes naturally, and this book will help you to achieve greater performance. If coaching is new to you, this book will help set new ways of thinking, about management, about performance, and about people. There will be some guide lines in which you can begin your practice.

There is no right way to coach, this book is a road map for you to decide which way you want to go, in coaching. You decide the route that you will take to achieve your goals. Your road map is your territory, you decide the landscape that it will have. The details of your landscape can turn people management into an art form, that is unique.

Given the crisis that we face, in terms of economic and leadership failures that are apparent, in the world today, coaching can help with the development of sound leadership. In practice coaching is not teaching, but setting the conditions for growing and learning. Coaching is setting the conditions for success, not failure.

M A. Grant

Chapter 1

What is Coaching

When I first started my research, career and passion for leadership, I discovered that 'coaching' would often appear, and not from a sporting context, which it is most commonly associated with. Early on I discovered as whilst attending a course conducted by a coaching consultant, that coaching was a leadership style, before I had undertaken the research I would have previously suggested that it was "leadership and coaching."

Coaching is now the must-have skill for the modern leader or manager, and if you have ever applied for a job recently you will notice that it has appeared on most job descriptions, finding its way in to Key Performance

Indicators (KPIs). But what was coaching?

There seems to be an abundance of books written on coaching, and depending on which book you read would determine the coaching style that would be adopted. There are thousands of training companies that are willing to take your money, all professing to be 'gurus' in coaching, and that in one or two days they could get you at the top of the coaching game.

For me this is concerning, since if they were this good at coaching, then there would be no need to take my hard earned cash for two days they would be delivering this in business themselves, as this is where the perception of money is.

If you looked for individuals that coach for performance within businesses and organizations, the list of coaches shortens, as most coaches work around the model of life coaching. Life coaching is a different style of coaching compared to coaching for performance within industry.

If you were the CEO of a large organization looking to implement coaching would you want an individual with no commercial experience that was very young coaching your company? The coaches have to start somewhere, but after a two day course the training companies that train these coaches, convince them that they are now equipped to take on this role. Most coaches that coach in performance usually make the step into coaching having previously held positions of authority in industry.

When I started to research coaching I discovered that a number of individuals and books would reference Sir Jon

Whitmore and the GROW tool, which is covered later in this book, as the basic or primary coaching tool. It would be wrong not to recommend this tool too.

I have been lucky enough to have met Sir John on a number of occasions. He was an invited member to an executive committee for one of my previous employers. In this chapter I will explain what coaching is, and in real terms how to use it for performance.

History

Coaching takes its origins from the English term "coach", which is derived from a medium of transport that traces its origins to the Hungarian word *kocsi* meaning "carriage" that was named after the village "Kocs" where it was first made.

The first use of the term coaching to mean an instructor or trainer arose around 1830 in Oxford University slang for a tutor who "carries" a student through an exam. Coaching thus has been used in language to describe the process used to transport people from where they are to where they want to be. The first use of the term in relation to sports came in the late 1800's.

Historically the evolution of coaching has been influenced by many other fields of study including those of personal development, adult education, psychology (sports, clinical, developmental, organizational, social and industrial) and other organizational or leadership theories and practices. Since the mid-1990s, coaching has developed into a more independent discipline and professional associations such as the Association for Coaching, and the European Coaching and Mentoring Council have helped develop a set of training standards.

Definition

Like all styles of leadership, and skills that you may use or new concepts, you have to come up with a definition, you have to define what it is that you are doing, for what purpose? Therefore it is important to determine the definition of coaching.

The UK Government use the following definition to explain coaching: "Coaching is the key to unlocking potential in order to maximize performance." You could 'Google' coaching definitions until you seem to find the one that fits for you if required.

I like this one as it has the key elements that have been designed to fit in the Value Based Leadership (VBL) model that is covered in a later chapter, which is potential and performance. Coaching is about taking potential and turning it into performance. Certainly within industry, organizations are looking for performance, which they can look to get return on any investment made. This definition is also in line with what Gallwey had suggested in the inner game.

I had been coaching this for a long time but hadn't realized this is was what I had been doing, I hadn't realized that I had been 'coaching', it was something that I had just done. If you think about this I have just given the definition, but what did we do before called it coaching? How did we get performance out of individuals or organizations without coaching?

Of course we did coach this, we just didn't call it coaching, we may have called it common sense or something similar, but it is important to note that coaching isn't something new. Individuals and organizations have been doing it for a long time, achieving some credible results. Later I will cover "goals", but what did we do before the word "goal" was used?

We still set goals, just under a different name. Perhaps the process had always been there, the language over time has changed. Anyone who has children will appreciate that they speak a completely different language now compared to when we were young, (lol, gr8, m8[1]).

Coaching then, is the way by which the best organisations aim to help people change their attitude and develop a positive psychology, and help them to become more confident and motivated, deal with stress, and maintain a positive mental attitude.

This is the philosophy of coaching, which suggests that irrespective of the knowledge and skills a person might have, they will only ever be able to perform their best by maintaining a positive mental attitude. In this way, coaching can be considered the key to "unlocking a person's potential to maximise their own performance".

In order to be truly effective, meanwhile, it is essential that every coach develops their own knowledge, skills and

---

[1] Laugh out Loud, Great and Mate.

attitude along these lines, not only with regards to coaching but also performance psychology.

Types of Coaching

There are many types of coaching that are used in the modern world, that all have their respective part to play. Its therefore important that you have an understanding of each one, some examples are as follows:

Personal/Life Coaching

The personal/life coach helps individuals gain awareness of and clarify their personal goals and priorities, better understand their thoughts, feelings, and options, and take appropriate actions to change their lives, accomplish their goals, and feel more fulfilled.

Career Coaching

The career coach helps individuals identify what they want and need from their career, then make decisions and take the needed actions to accomplish their career objectives in balance with the other parts of their lives.

Group Coaching

Group coaches work with individuals in groups. The focus can range from leadership development to career development, stress management to team building. Group coaching combines the benefits of individual coaching with the resources of groups. Individuals learn from each other and the interactions that take place within the group setting.

Performance Coaching

Performance coaches help employees at all levels better understand the requirements of their jobs, the competencies needed to fulfil those requirements, any gaps in their current performance, and opportunities to improve performance. Coaches then work with the employees, their bosses, and others in their workplace to help the employees fill performance gaps and develop plans for further professional development.

Newly Assigned Leader Coaching

Coaches of individuals assigned or hired into new leadership roles help these leaders to "onboard". The goal of the coaching is to clarify with the leader's key constituents the most important responsibilities of her new role, her deliverables in the first few months of the new assignment, and ways to integrate the team she will lead with the organization. The major focus of this type of coaching is on helping the new leader to assimilate and achieve her business objectives.

Relationship Coaching

The relationship coach helps two or more people to form, change, or improve their interactions. The context can be work, personal, or other settings.

High-Potential or Developmental Coaching

The coach works with organizations to develop the potential of individuals who have been identified as key to the organization's future or are part of the organization's succession plan. The focus of the coaching may include assessment, competency development, or assistance planning and implementing strategic projects.

Coaching to Provide Feedback Debriefing and Development

Planning Organizations that use assessment or 360 feedback processes often utilize coaches to help employees interpret the results of their assessments and feedback. In addition, coaches work with individuals to make career decisions and establish professional development plans based on feedback, assessment results, and other relevant data.

Targeted Behavioural Coaching

Coaches who provide targeted behavioural coaching help individuals to change specific behaviours or habits or learn new, more effective ways to work and interact with others. This type of coaching often helps individuals who are otherwise very successful in their current jobs or are taking on new responsibilities that require a change in specific behaviours.

Legacy Coaching

The legacy coach helps leaders who are retiring from a key role to decide on the legacy they would like to leave behind. The coach also provides counsel on transitioning out of the leadership role.

Succession Coaching

The succession coach helps assess potential candidates for

senior management positions and prepares them for promotion to more senior roles. This type of coaching may be used in any organization that is experiencing growth or turnover in its leadership ranks. It is especially helpful in family businesses to maintain the viability of the firm. Since assessment is often part of this intervention, clear expectations and ground rules for confidentiality are essential. It may be necessary in some companies to use separate consultants for assessment and coaching.

Presentation/Communication Skills Coaching

This type of coaching helps individuals gain self-awareness about how they are perceived by others and why they are perceived in that way. Clients learn new ways to interact with others. The use of video recording with feedback allows clients to see themselves as others do. The coach helps clients change the way they communicate and influence others by changing their words, how they say those words, and the body language they use to convey their intended messages.

Team Coaching

One or more team coaches work with the leader and members of a team to establish their team mission, vision, strategy, and rules of engagement with one another. The team leader and members may be coached individually to facilitate team meetings and other interactions, build the effectiveness of the group as a high-performance team, and achieve team goals.

Mentoring

Although this book focuses on coaching, it is worth touching on mentoring, as it is sometimes linked. The approach of mentoring is to develop the whole person and so the techniques are broad and require wisdom in order to be used appropriately. The mentor is normally an expert in the field that they are mentoring in to a mentee.

The five most commonly used techniques among mentors were:

Accompanying making a commitment in a caring way, which involves taking part in the learning process side-by-side with the learner.

Sowing: mentors are often confronted with the difficulty of preparing the learner before he or she is ready to change. Sowing is necessary when you know that what you say may not be understood or even acceptable to learners at first but will make sense and have value to the mentee when the situation requires it.

Catalyzing: when change reaches a critical level of pressure, learning can escalate. Here the mentor chooses to plunge the learner right into change, provoking a different way of thinking, a change in identity or a re-ordering of values.

Showing: this is making something understandable, or using your own example to demonstrate a skill or activity. You show what you are talking about, you show by your own behavior.

Harvesting: here the mentor focuses on "picking the ripe fruit": it is usually used to create awareness of what was learned by experience and to draw conclusions. The key questions here are: "What have you learned?", "How useful is it?".

Different techniques may be used by mentors according to the situation and the mindset of the mentee, and the techniques used in modern organizations can be found in ancient education systems, from the Socratic technique of harvesting to the accompaniment method of learning used in the apprenticeship of itinerant cathedral builders during the Middle Ages. I often advise mentors to look for "teachable moments" in order to "expand or realize the potentialities of the people in the organizations they lead" and underline that personal credibility is as essential to quality mentoring as skill.

Multiple Mentors A new and upcoming trend is having multiple mentors. This can be helpful because we can all learn from each other. Having more than one mentor will widen the knowledge of the person being mentored. There are different mentors who may have different strengths.

Profession or Trade Mentor: This is someone who is currently in the trade/profession you are entering. They know the trends, important changes and new practices that you should know to stay at the top of your career. A mentor like this would be someone you can discuss ideas regarding the field, and also be introduced to key and important people that you should know.

Industry Mentor: This is someone who doesn't just focus on the profession. This mentor will be able to give insight on the industry as a whole. Whether it be research, development or key changes in the industry, you need to know.

Organization Mentor: Politics in the organizations are constantly changing. It is important to be knowledgeable about the values, strategies and products that are within your company, but also when these things are changing. An organization mentor can clarify missions and strategies, and give clarity when needed.

Work Process Mentor: This mentor can speed quickly over the bumps, and cut through the unnecessary work. This mentor can explain the 'ins and outs' of projects, day to day tasks, and eliminate unnecessary things that may be currently going on in your work day. This mentor can help to get things done quickly and efficiently.

Technology Mentor: This is an up-and-coming, incredibly important position. Technology has been rapidly improving, and becoming more a part of day to day transactions within companies. In order to perform your best, you must know how to get things done on the newest technology. A technology mentor will help with technical breakdowns, advise on systems that may work better than what you're currently using, and coach you through new technology and how to best use it and implement it into your daily life.

These mentors are only examples. There can be many more different types of mentors. Look around your workplace, your life, and see who is an expert that you can learn something from. The rest of this book will focus on coaching, but mentoring certainly works alongside coaching.

Code of Conduct

Within coaching if you are looking to make it a career or you have been doing this for some time, then having guidelines is a great way to ensure that you have consistency in your coaching with all coaches.

Within an organisation set up, if coaching is taking place then there should be an internal policy on the coaching standards to be adopted. A suggested code of conduct that the European Coaching & Mentoring Council (EMCC) recommend[2] is located at the back of the book.

---

[2] Current as of 2015

M A. Grant

Chapter 2 – Leadership

What is Leadership?

What is leadership? What does the word leadership mean? We often say we use it; some even think they are experts at using it. Early in my career, I responsible for the leadership delivery, implementation and instruction, at a UK Government Leadership School. At that time I was undertaking the start of my academic journey, and I noticed the sheer vastness of leadership literature out there. Which leadership model is the right one to adopt? If you were to search for "leadership books" in Amazon, you get over twenty-two thousand hits.

Most people can talk about leadership, but few really understand it; most people want to achieve it. When you start to examine it, it always surprises me how quickly one word can illicit such an emotional response in people. Right now as you are reading this, you will be having an internal emotional debate, already talking to yourself, explaining that you already know what leadership is. You are drawing from your past experiences and formulating your own internal model of it.

The first thing that I suggest, is to define what leadership is, in order to position coaching within. Here is a group activity that you can try – use a flip chart and ask the group to come with a definition of leadership. Get the group to write down their individual group definitions. Then have a look at the definitions that the group give. You will rarely get any two groups with the same definition.

This is the difficulty in trying to define leadership. This was a puzzle for me too. How can you define something that has so many different meanings to so many people and organizations, especially if they have been exposed to different styles of leadership in the past.

The next time you walk into a book shop, go to the business section and look up books on leadership, there will be several leadership books that all explain what leadership is. How do you define the leadership that will work for you? Which model of leadership would be the best one to adopt?

There has been previous academic research that had taken place in aligning leadership and the values of the organization (Hardy and Arthur, 2006) leading to examination of the results in relation to performance. This is key for me, as I in coaching I look to increase performance.

Values Based Leadership

The leadership school mentioned earlier, would go on to define leadership as Values Based Leadership (VBL). This term VBL would form the model of leadership I would go on to adopt. Before I can explain what VBL is we need to examine what is a value, and why they are important within leadership?

Understanding what a value is was important in understanding the model VBL. It is important to understand a little of the leadership thinking that has got me to the VBL model and the learning that got me there on my leadership journey. This will place in the foundations to understanding the leadership secret.

Values

What do you think of when someone asks you to name an example of a value? I have often asked myself the same question and I'm sure that like me you think the traditional values that are commonly mentioned such as loyalty, discipline, integrity and love as examples.

It turns out that values are the specific belief systems that we have about that which is most important to us. Here is the first dilemma in setting values: you have to be honest with yourself, and if you're not honest with yourself then you cannot place value on your own values. Asking yourself to be honest is difficult, as you may not like your own answer.

They are the fundamental, ethical, moral and practical judgments that we make about what is right and wrong. This is our internal moral compass and it guides us accordingly. As such, values direct our motivation and, in the same way, can be described as either toward or away from. Similarly, whether operating at the conscious level or unconscious level, they guide our every decision and ultimately determine our behaviour and results.

This was a very important discovery, that values could have an impact on results, and our behaviour towards them. My behaviour has changed over a period of leadership development, and academic learning. This must mean that my values had to have changed too, in order to get the change in behaviour.

What happens, however, if you do not have a clear idea as to what is most important to yourself and what your values are? As a result of this you may do things and, then afterwards, you find that you are unhappy with yourself. This is a type of "internal conflict" that arises because of opposing sets of values that conflict with each other. Although you might take action at one level (conscious), there is a part of you (unconscious) that does not believe that what you are doing is right.

This type of internal conflict invariably results in failure and you end up feeling bad about yourself. How many times have you not really tried at something and then, when you don't get the result, you feel bad about yourself? Not about the result but knowing you could have done better yourself. This is often the case at work, at school and or perhaps going to the gym as an example.

In order to get the results that we want in our lives, we have to have a clear and fundamental sense of who we are, what really matters. This is all pretty straight forward, but how do we get our employees to take on the values if the organization doesn't believe in them themselves? This is going to have a direct impact on the performance of the company.

This reminds me of a time I was asked to look at the results of a large organization within the United Arab Emirates (UAE) for a large government company. They had invested considerable money in the creation of their values and the behaviours that they wanted but weren't getting the behaviour from their majority of the staff. When I looked into this, I discovered that the values and the behaviours that they had designed were functional and relevant to the company and designed well.

The issue I discovered was that although the senior management had all the relevant training, and understood the values and behaviours, similar training had not been delivered to the majority of the work force. It had been disseminated by internal email or marketing that most employees hadn't seen or taken any notice of.

My advice to them was that they didn't need me at all that, in order to see the behaviour desired they had to first disseminate the values by training to all members of staff, in the similar fashion that they had given to the senior management. This was common sense, but was now asking some difficult questions of the organization – such as did they truly value their own workforce? If they did they wouldn't have needed me to show them.

The key then is getting individuals to connect to the values, especially if companies values are different to that of the individual. What is needed is that emotional connection to the value. I often see this in values, that although they have been designed well, the relevance and dissemination within the company has not been thought about in the same detail. I have also seen too often companies getting the behaviour mixed up with the values. This has an effect when the value is the behaviour, not a value.

Beliefs

Linking values to our behaviours are our beliefs, what are our beliefs? Research suggests beliefs are the knowledge structures, located in the brain memory, that contain our experience of ourselves, other people, and the world in which we live. As such, they give us a sense of certainty in an uncertain world, allowing us to anticipate what will happen in given situations, and guide and facilitate our behaviour.

Values, meanwhile, are the specific belief systems we have about what is most important to us, and incorporate the fundamental, ethical, moral and practical judgments we make about what is right and wrong. Fundamentally, these things not only determine who we are, but what we are capable of. We therefore have a vested interest in understanding them so that we can control them rather than have them control us.

Armed with this definition of values and beliefs, it was important that I understand what effect beliefs could have on performance, and all of the books that I had been reading at that time suggested that these beliefs are split into limiting and empowering beliefs.

Empowering and Limiting Beliefs

It occurred to me, that our beliefs play an important role in determining our performance, so I looked at some successful individuals and what made them successful. I couldn't imagine Richard Branson sat there at the beginning and thinking that he was going to fail, when he created the Virgin brand.

Imagine a football manager addressing their team prior to a big game, coming off the back of a previous loss. Although they have just had a negative result, they don't plan on getting another failure, the address to the team is still about winning the next game, it's about planning for success and not failure.

People who succeed in life differ greatly in their beliefs from those that fail. Our beliefs about who we are, and who we can be, determine what we will be. If we believe in a life of opportunity, we invariably live a life of opportunity. If we believe our life is defined by narrow limits, then we invariably make those limits real.

What we believe to be true or possible becomes what is true or possible. It is an example of the self-fulfilling cycle; if I believe I won't or can't then I don't get the results. If I believe I can I am more likely to succeed, even if I don't get the initial results I'm looking for, I accept that I will get them.

I would go on to understand the difference between limiting and empowering beliefs. Beliefs can either be empowering or limiting. Whilst an empowering belief is one that facilitates our happiness, growth, and fulfilment, a limiting belief inevitably stops us from realizing our true potential.

We can usually identify which of our beliefs are empowering and limiting by reflecting upon the language that we use to describe them. Typically we describe our empowering beliefs in terms of "I'm good at", "I like" or "I can". Similarly, we usually describe our limiting beliefs in terms of "I'm no good at", "I don't like" and "I can't."

If I can understand that these powerful beliefs were linked to my values I could use this information to impact on performance? If I knew that I had a limiting belief, what could I do to change it into a empowering belief? Similarly, if an organization is made up of a culture of it "can't be done", "it will never change", "we always do it that way". Then what could be done to change the belief system to that of a empowering one?

Later I would be in involved with a high performance organization that worked on a ten percent pass rate as its performance bench mark. They had approached me to increase the pass rate. I had started to dig into the organization and the beliefs and values that were evident.

I found that they believed that that they had always got a ten percent pass rate and that no matter what they did, they would always get a ten percent pass rate. They also believed that if the pass rate went up that they would be seen as the ones who had dropped the standard in order to increase the pass rate.

By addressing the beliefs and turning their limiting beliefs into empowering ones, demonstrating that there would be no drop in standard and that the results were performance driven, the organization was able to deliver an increase to a sixteen percent first time pass rate.

This sounded great, but caused a whole new set of issues, as the rest of the organization had only been preparing for the ten percent that they normally had passing, now there was an additional six percent, a nice problem to have though.

Leadership Thinking

I turned my attention to leadership, investigating leadership theory that had evolved over the years. In order to build up this knowledge I needed to understand how we had got to where we are today in current leadership thinking. I had to explore the theory of leadership thinking and discover where we are today in relation to this thinking.

I needed to research leadership history. This was daunting at first, as I had mentioned earlier, the amount of leadership literature that was out there. I started to ask other people that I respected about where did they go for references in their leadership development.

At times I got back the standard reply of 'erm uhm you know it's that thing, it's where we do this, where we do that.' Getting an answer on where I could go to research leadership history was equally as hard as asking what does the word leadership mean mentioned earlier.

I had to really search and seek out credible individuals that were impartial and not selling their own history or view of the history of leadership. Through this research I had managed to find the following snap shot of the history of leadership thinking, whilst remaining as impartial as possible without any bias:

Great Man – based on a belief that leaders are exceptional people born with innate qualities, destined to lead. If you study their lives you can emulate them. Problem is that great leaders such as Ghandi, Thatcher, Churchill and Mandela display widely different personal qualities. Studying a person is one thing, being able to copy them is another.

The Trait - approach abandons linking leadership qualities with particular individuals and lists a number of traits or characteristics which are believed to relate to effective leadership. However, studies have failed to find any link between effective leadership and any single characteristic.

Behaviourist - theories focus on what leaders really do and the differences between effective and non-effective leaders. This is an avenue where you can look at styles of leadership.

Situational - leadership is about the specific context in which leadership is being exercised. For example, military leadership may demand skills, qualities and behaviours which differ from those associated with leadership in industry.

Transactional - emphasizes the importance of the relationship between leaders and followers, focusing on the mutual benefits derived from a form of "contract" through which the leader delivers rewards or recognition in return for the commitment or loyalty of the followers. This is the most widely used leadership style and it seems the easiest one to adopt.

Transformational - theory, the central concept is still about a relationship between leader and led, but is about creating a vision, having shared values and obtaining commitment to change. Mutual trust is the key to being a transformational leader.

This was my brief glimpse into my research in leadership thinking. Modern examples of individuals that are linked to leadership success, are Gates, Jobbs and Branson to name but a few. There has been a shift to move away from the military leaders of the past, that were associated with leadership thinking.

Leadership Styles

It seemed that after taking a fast track look at leadership thinking I had ended up at transactional and transformation leadership; these were first identified by James McGregor Burns in 1978. They were spectrums of opposites on a scale on which you could place, leadership. Transactional leadership produces change at the psychological level of actions and results, to change what people "do".

Transformational leadership produces change at the

psychological level of values and beliefs to change how people "think". This level of change suggests that the person, not just their behaviour, has been changed or "transformed".

In order to get an idea for the spectrum of leadership styles through transactional and transformational leadership I found that six leadership styles (Daniel Goleman, 1990) were researched in having impact on the climate of an organization and of those being led.

Currently, transformational leadership is the buzz word within leadership, but was identified over three decades ago, and it is only now that individuals and organizations are looking to implement a wide spectrum of different styles in leadership. It highlights that if it has taken this long for them to wake up to the possibility of change within leadership how sometimes barriers that are evident during organizational change can take a long time to break down.

It is important at this stage to let you know that these styles of leadership that Goleman looked at are not the definitive styles of leadership, just examples of styles of leadership that fitted the best for the VBL model that was created. Language is important as they are examples 'of' and not 'the' examples. From a consultancy perspective, if there were others that fitted or seemed to fit a given situation, then these could have been adopted.

In order to develop VBL, it was important to look at the styles in more detail, since these styles form an important element in the VBL model, and similarly I had to explore them in the same way that I had approached the leadership thinking, whilst remaining impartial. It was important that I looked at them as individuals styles initially, and Goleman suggested the following styles, which I have expanded to fit in with the VBL model:

Directive Leadership: "Tell: Do what I tell you"

This leadership style demands immediate compliance from the work force or individuals. Certainly there is a feel of 'Just do it' – I'm the boss, there is little room for negotiation. Tight control is exercised by the leader. It involves a lot negative feedback – 'you didn't do that right'; which can often lead to a fear of failure syndrome.

This is not particularly useful if trying to implement a culture of change. It can result in new ideas being stifled; cooperation falls, and inflexibility is often evident.

That said, this style of leadership is a very good approach in a crisis situation with a competent team. You may have seen this style used by Sir Alan Sugar on the television show the Apprentice[3] – where he explains exactly what he wants to see.

Visionary or Authoritative Leadership: "Sell: Come with me"

This style of leadership mobilizes people towards a vision, it is firm but fair: "come with me" outlook. It is based on a development of a clear agreed vision, clear standards and feedback. It explains the rationale for procedures that need

---

[3] *The Apprentice* is a British reality game show in which a group of aspiring businessmen and women compete for the chance to work with the British business magnate Alan Sugar

to be adopted within the organization or by the individual. It can be motivating; as it explains the 'why' but leaves the 'how' to team members.

This is very empowering for the team members. Praise outweighs criticism, with clear meaningful goals established from the beginning with long term direction. Team members see how their task fits into the bigger picture. This style of leadership is a favourite with film makers, as when linked to music it can produce powerful emotions. Who can forget the opening words to a very successful film and television franchise - "Space, the final frontier…"[4]

Pacesetting leadership: "Do as I do, now!" - or I'll do it myself."

In this particular style the team leader sets high standards for performance, and leads by example. Subordinates are unlikely to innovate incase the standards fall and the task s taken from them. As a result of this there is often reluctant delegation with an obsession about doing things better, faster and quicker. It does, however, pinpoint poor performance and then as a result it can eradicate it.

A pacesetters demand for excellence can sometimes overwhelm a number of team members as sometimes there is a thought that although they can do that, there is no way that I will be able to do it. Poor performance is normally not tolerated, with any form of praise rarely used.

There is not normally any vision created, and it looks

---

[4] Star Trek

towards the short term only. Because of this there is a tendency to be a lack of coordination, which often means that the big picture is lost.

One of the ways that I picture this style of leadership is on some sort of instruction as if you are part of a well-oiled machine, perhaps learning to be a fireman for example, where you are taught a little, practice a little, and so on. Evident during instructor lead teaching for a new skill.

Affiliative Leadership: "People first, task second"

This style of leadership creates harmony and strong emotional bonds. Often though there is a lack of challenge that is then compromised by the desire to keep other team members happy. Harmony within the team ends up more important than standards. This can have a direct impact on performance.

With the affiliative style there is usually undifferentiated praise given, and this is normally for fear of upsetting another team member. Little explanation on direction or rationale behind tasks is given as focus on praise can allow poor performance to go unchecked. In organizations that adopt this style, standards may be low so all can achieve the required performance. A lack of clear advice or direction can leave team members floundering.

I often reflect thinking that this type of leadership, when used, reminds me more of a conversation. Think about how you would build relationships and rapport with people. How did your weekend go? Is your wife feeling better? And so on.

Participative Leadership: "What do you think?"

This style of leadership uses the 'what do you think?' approach where by ideas are encouraged on a grand scale; collaboration and team agreement is often sought out. There is a need for consensus, which may compromise effort and success within the team. Because there is a high reliance on trust, respect and commitment this can lead to decisions being delayed for too long until central agreements can be reached.

Because everyone is involved they all share the rewards, and this then discourages differential discretionary effort. There is a tendency for this style to lead to confusion and lack of direction in time of crisis

Certain government styles of council will often practice this style of leadership. As will meetings at boardroom level within industry.

Coaching leadership: "What if you could?" Or "Try this" or "Ask, don't tell"

This style of leadership is covered in the next chapter, but in essence it encourages dialogue within the organization and looks to the future. It involves developing others, and does not assume one 'font of all knowledge' for everyone. The leaders will help other team members to discover their own strengths and weaknesses, and as a result will develop specific needs.

This will sometimes lead to standards dropping in the short term whilst team members 'try things out' and develop the required new skills.

There has to be regular feedback and positive reinforcement throughout and the delivery of the feedback is key – there is a real sense that team leaders care about the future of their workforce. The long term development and future-proofing is important, which leads to it being adapted to fit other parts of the organization.

Initially it may be a time consuming style and it needs a degree of expertise from the leader, which has to be taught or developed. There may be some instances of team members being very resistant to learning or changing or developing as they may see this as a threat.

Individuals find it strange that one of the people who emphasizes the hard edges of the coaching style is Gordon Ramsay[5]. Many people would associate him with the more coercive elements, but if you look at what he does when he is in a kitchen, there is a huge amount of really honest feedback. He thinks about people's vision for their restaurant and helps them to reach their goals; it is not about him saying what he would do.

Another thing about coaching as a leadership style is the fact that we use it as a leadership style. Often people refer to leadership and coaching or management and coaching, but I had realized earlier that it is not the case, it is just a part of leadership. A training company won't tell you this as this is one of the ways that they make more money out of selling you training programs that you don't really need based in leadership and management.

---

[5] Gordon Ramsay is known for presenting TV programs about competitive cookery and food, such as the British series *Hell's Kitchen*, *The F Word*, and *Ramsay's Kitchen Nightmares*

The Golf Bag

In order to contextualize these leaderships styles together for this example, I'm going to use the six styles that was suggested earlier, that have been briefly explained. We have to determine which one is the best? The title of the book is based on a leadership secret, so here is a little secret on the styles of leadership that you won't find in any of the books or with the consultants you may have come across.

Certainly, at the moment coaching is a strong 'buzz' word, so if you are talking to a coach they of course are going to suggest that coaching would be the most appropriate one to use. In fact, the secret of any leadership style is that they all work, they all get results! But which one to use, and when to use it?

Imagine now, that you are a top golfer, and you're playing in the United States PGA Open. You are standing on the first tee and the green is some five hundred and seventy five yards away. Don't worry if you have never played before, just picture that you need to take the biggest club out of the golf bag and hit the ball as hard as you can, and as straight as you can.

You address the ball[6] and hit it as hard as you can, unfortunately, although you hit it over three hundred yards, it falls to the right in the long grass.

As you walk up to the ball, having spent ten minutes searching for it, you now have to get the golf ball back on

---

[6] Golfing terminology.

to the fairway. So you need select a smaller club from the golf bag. You hit the ball out of the long grass, but although you are progressing towards the green you land in a bunker, which is full of sand.

Now you need to look into the golf bag, and take out the club that has been specially designed to get the ball out of the sand. Again you address the ball and you manage to hit it out of the sand and it lands on the green. Inside the golf bag is a club called a putter that has been designed so you can tap the ball into the hole. After three taps you manage to get the ball into the hole.

What has this got to do with our leadership styles? The way I approach this, is that we carry around with us a leadership "golf bag", and I need to stress again that no single style is thought to be the best, but like a good golfer the good leader varies appropriate style according to situation and team member concerned. Just the same way that you would select the club as mentioned earlier, to get the golf ball into the hole.

Thinking about this Golf Club analogy – what is your most effective leadership club? In other words, what is the most effective 'club' you have in your leadership golf bag? Which one do you understand the most? Which one do you least understand?

The thing to remember is: whether playing golf or leading – we need to get results, by selecting the most appropriate golf club (leadership style), that we need to get the ball into the hole. It just happens that the coaching style is the one that is least understood, with the direct style being the traditionally easier one to adopt.

Values Based Leadership

If I now go back to VBL, and how it was created, what does it look like? How can we use VBL? In order to demonstrate VBL you need to think about the behaviours that you want from an organization. For this example I am going to construct the metaphor of a building, and build the VBL model around it.

Once we have these behaviours, they can be placed at the top of the building. The values are placed at the bottom. Imagine a house with the roof acting as the behaviours and the values as the foundations. Supporting walls need to be created to ensure that the building will stand up, these are our leadership styles.

In essence we have our behaviours, which are taken from the leadership style that is adopted, which is underpinned by the values, hence the term Values Based Leadership. The point is, that if we were to look down on top of the building, the part that we see is the behaviour.

VBL is based on strong foundations that enable the wanted behaviours to be applied, using the appropriate leadership style to fit each unique situation. As these styles are used as a "skill" they can be each developed, and performance improved in each.

Representation of Values Based Leadership:

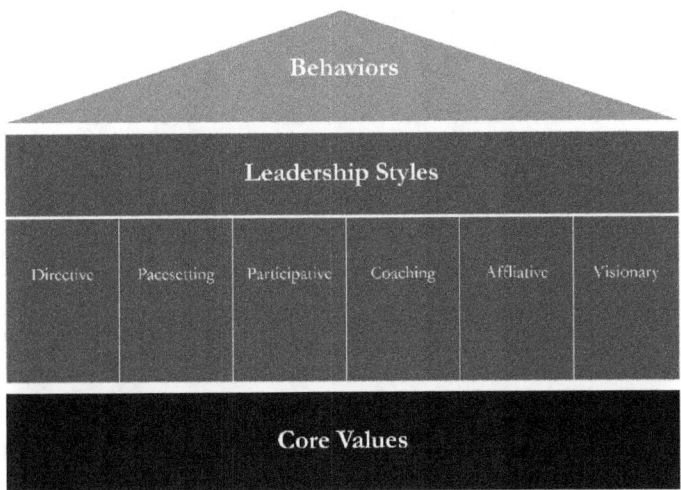

If we are feeling stressed we would normally revert to the style of leadership that we feel most comfortable with. Ask yourself which style of leadership do you feel most comfortable using from the examples given earlier? Which style do you think you see most when people or organizations are stressed?

Nine times out of ten it's going to be more of a transactional style from the spectrum of those styles. They are the most easily adopted. Here then is the thing though: they all get results, it doesn't matter which style that is adopted, they all get results. Some may get you results quicker, some may get you there with more empowerment, some may get you there with an angry workforce.

It doesn't matter, they will all eventually bring you the result; it's how you get there that is really important. The more transformational styles such as coaching are great for results but are the least understood.

Having completed research into different styles of leadership, I was now satisfied with the concept of leadership related to the model of VBL, and the leadership thinking that got me there, I was also armed with my leadership golf bag.

I know that by asking these questions of myself within the VBL model, I was comfortable with the transactional styles, but now realized that I was not so comfortable with the coaching styles. I needed to fully understand them and develop them so that I felt equally comfortable. I needed to get on the leadership driving range and reduce my leadership handicap.[7]

The Leadership Secret

I have now shown you how leadership thinking ended up with the VBL model. The thing is not to say that VBL is the definitive leadership theory, of course not, it is a blend of leadership theories that fit where we are today in current leadership thinking linked to values and behaviours.

If I think back to when my grandparents were young I think that they had a stronger values set than that of the

---

[7] Golfing analogy to reduce your score and increase performance.

majority of young people now. Society has changed, technology is changing every day, perhaps there wasn't a need for VBL in the past. But today, in a world that is ever shrinking, how do we ensure common values and shared goals in our organizations?

VBL plays a part in aligning this and ensuring performance in the workplace. Imagine a large multinational company that recruits from all over the world: all the employees bring with them a value set from their respective countries and cultures, however, when they work at the company they are expected to behave in a way that supports the values of the company. When we place this together we have the leadership secret, the ugly truth.

The leadership secret is, that there is no secret. We want to imagine that there is something fundamentally concrete at the end of the explanation. The truth is that when it comes down to it, leadership is just you, plain and simple.

M A. Grant

Chapter 3 – The Coaching Process

The Coaching Process

In order to more formalise coaching, its order to consider the creation of a process, on which to anchor coaching. This process will ensure that, if followed, proven results can be achieved if combined with the skills and tools that align to it.

What would happen if there was no process to follow? What would the results be? Imagine now that the factory that produces "Ford" cars, as an example, does not follow a set process. What would the "Ford" product look like at the end of the process? Would the consumer get, what they were after? Of course not, this is the same within coaching. If there is no set process to follow, how can we achieve any credible results.

It was important in my coaching development, that I followed a recognised or proven process. This process that would be adopted, needed to support coaching tools such as the GROW[8] tool, it should fit over most things that we do in the workplace, but adapted for coaching.

The process that was created starts at the bottom and the works upwards like climbing a ladder, and in order to get to the top you need to complete each step, and if you try to skip a step you could slip, or if not taken properly you could slip therefore it is important to take the logical steps, the process is as follows:

Raise Awareness: The beginning step of the coaching process is raising awareness. During this initial step you have to help the person or organization to create a vision of their goal (objective) in terms of what they want to achieve, what would be a reason to why they might want to achieve it? How do they intend to do so?

It is important that throughout this first step that the emphasis is on guiding the person or individual towards finding their own solutions to their own performance problems. Particularly for an individuals or organization, as it works for both. In this way, raising awareness is about getting the person to think for themselves for the act of raising the awareness. If you end up having to tell rather than ask then the goal is normally your goal and not theirs, and for this reason they have to come up with it for themselves.

---

[8] Covered in the chapter 7.

Generate Responsibility: The next step of the coaching process is to get the person or organization to generate responsibility. During this step it is important to challenge the person or organization to take action towards making their goal a reality. In this way, generating responsibility is about getting the person or organization to feel they want to achieve it for themselves.

If they are unwilling to do this then they are not going to really want to do it. If there is a problem in generating responsibility, then you may have to go back to raising awareness. You cannot progress to the next step in the process without generating responsibility.

Facilitate Performance: The next step in the process is to facilitate the performance of the individual or organization. This usually takes place inside the workplace. During this step the idea is to support the person or organization as they take action towards making their goal a reality and deals with the challenge of doing so. In this way, facilitating performance is about getting the person to do for themselves.

This performance step is where all the magic happens, and I learned that in order to make the difference and allow training transfer it has to happen in the workplace. Have you ever been on a training course when the trainer then follow you back to the work place to ensure that you were then carrying out the actions taught from the course?

Training Transfer

If you have to attend a course there should be at least an

additional day for the follow up to ensure that this training transfer has taken place, it is also a great way to measure performance. In this way I learned that in order to get the performance

I had to go into the workplace and ensure training transfer was taking place, and from a coaching point of view, you cannot progress to the performance step until the first two have been climbed. If you do, you are probably not going to get the desired result or performance.

If you think about it logically, these three steps can be placed over most things in life or work. Imagine you want to bring in a new Human Resource (HR) system: the first thing you are going to do is raise awareness to the new system, and the part that everyone has to play in it. You would then have to generate responsibility for those people who are going to be using the system or involved in it.

Finally there will be the performance of using the new system. I can remember when I was younger, having had a new HR system that was to be implemented, and thinking that it will never work, but I was told that I was to use them anyway. After a period of time I realized that I had to use it, and then once I had accepted it became workable.

If I had got the first two steps in first I would have come to the same conclusion only earlier, which means the performance would have been achieved earlier. In business terms this would start to affect the bottom line.

This process is nothing new, we have been going through this process for some time. People who "coached", but did not necessarily know that they were coaching, or organisations that were going through organisational change, will go through this process. It's the what if scenario? What happens if we don't raise the awareness or generate responsibility? We can still get the results by adopting a more transactional style of leadership, but will the results be as good as if individuals or organisations take control for their own performance.

If I make my children, sit and order them to do their homework, they will do their homework, they will submit any homework as per deadlines that may be given. But if the children can get to the taking responsibility stage, then in theory they should get better results?

In order to facilitate this performance using this process, as a coach we need to be armed with the right skill set...

M A. Grant

Chapter 4 – Coaching Skills

Goals

What is a goal? How many times have you heard this word used in the modern workplace, or even in the home? "What is a goal?" is fundamental as it turns out that goal setting is the key to successful performance, and it's the primary tool for getting results.

A goal can be described as whatever a person is trying to accomplish, the aim, object or target of their actions. This means that our goals typically relate to the achievement of a specific outcome or result, that which a person "wants", and usually involves a specific timeframe.

Goal setting, meanwhile, refers to the process of setting goals. It suggests that there is a specific method for getting the results we want. This is true if we look at following our dreams and having aspirations as forms of goal setting, but these processes are much more intuitive than proper goal setting.

By turning our dreams and aspirations into goals, and following the goal setting process, we are much better placed to turn our goals into reality. We could spend the first half of our lives thinking this is what I want to achieve, and the second half thinking I wish I had achieved this.

I have discovered, that there are generally three types of goals that are important in the process of goal setting, and these can be used independently or they can be used in conjunction with one another, these are:

Outcome goals: These goals usually relate to the dreams and aspirations from which the goal originated and are often expressed as a mission statement or vision. They are usually described subjectively in terms of emotion and are concerned with why the goal is important. Outcome goals are important for motivation and commitment.

Performance goals: These goals relate to a predetermined standard against which achievement can be measured. They are described objectively in terms of cognition and are concerned with what the goal actually is. Performance goals are very important for focus, control and recognition of goal attainment.

Process goals: These goals relate to what needs to be done in order to make the goal a reality. They are described prescriptively in terms of behaviour and are concerned with how the goal actually is to be achieved.

Large process goals are normally broken down into interim or sub goals. Process goals are important for monitoring what works and what doesn't work.

SMART Principles

Smarter principles, or SMART, is a useful tool that aids in ensuring that the goal is achieved. You will have noticed that SMART is now used in the workplace, and it is commonly used outside of coaching terms, which is testament to the fact that SMART works, but what does it stand for and how do we make it smarter?

I would have liked to take the credit for this but this is all down to Sir John Whitmore, and it is still as relevant today as it was when he first published it.

The acronym SMART is a useful tool with which to remember the fundamental principles of effective goal setting, exploring our goals more fully, and ensuring that they are clearly and precisely defined as possible. They are as follows:

Specific: Goals should be always be clearly and positively defined in terms that are behavioural. In this way, they should relate to outcomes and actions that are specific rather than ones that are general. Rather than simply saying that we are going to be a better manager or that we are going to get fitter, we should be looking to describe in exactly what way we are going to be a better manager and in exactly what way we are going to get fitter.

An example I get with young graduates is that they want to be the CEO. I then have to dig down to make it as specific as possible, the CEO of what organization? Which company do you want to be the CEO of? Otherwise it ends up being just a general comment, 'I want to be a CEO.'

Measurable: Goals should be measurable, such that they set a benchmark, that can be used to monitor progress. In order to do so, we should be asking ourselves how we will know when we are a better manager? How will we know when we are fitter?

If we look at the goal setting process as a path that we intend to follow, we need to know where the path starts and where the path ends. We also need to have established milestones along the way, in order to ensure that we are not deviating from the path that we have chosen.

Look at the CEO comment, how could this be measured? If I am dealing with graduates, and the goal is to be the CEO of a specific company, one way that could demonstrate the measure: is in the form of promotions. Each promotion would stack up and demonstrate that the goal is measurable. In the workplace, the achievement of KPIs could also serve as a measure of performance.

Achievable: Many people or organizations set goals that are completely out of reach for them or knowingly impossible to achieve. Although this practice is clearly self-defeating, many people do this in order to have a built-in excuse for not achieving their goals.

We must always have a realistic chance of reaching our goals, combined with a belief that we can reach them, in order to stay committed to them. This is the essence of "realistic" goal setting, although we must be careful how we use this term, extraordinary things are not achieved by realistic people!

Take the graduate again. It would be perfectly feasible that if they are young and just starting in the company that the position of CEO is attainable, however, if an individual's is in their mid-fifties and they are starting at the bottom of the company and it takes on average 35 years to become the CEO, then this specific goal may not be attainable. The use of goal setting is a powerful tool in the management of expectations.

Repeatable: Fundamentally, performance and achievement are a process of "constant and never-ending improvement." As such, our goals should reflect this by being long-term. Short-term and intermediate goals (sub-goals), meanwhile, provide useful "stepping stones" that can help us to maintain our focus.

In order to do this, however, our goals not only have to be measurable – they need to be repeatable too. This also helps in monitoring our progress towards our goals. The graduate looking at promotion in the forms of measure, what steps did they take to achieve the first promotion?

If they then repeat these actions then the second promotion should follow, as I have demonstrated a proven action and performance. Could you also use this in another part of the workplace to repeat performance? When results come in and are repeatable they can spread very quickly and an organization can add substantial increases to the bottom line through repeatable performance.

Timed: In order for our goals to be measured in any real way they need to be timed. All too often individuals and organizations have goals that they are going to commit to "someday". Goals such as these are very rarely achieved, and certainly not within the timeframe originally intended.

GOAL Setting

In order to help set GOALs that are SMART then the following process can be followed:

Define the goal and develop a strategy: The first stage requires that we decide upon both our goal and our strategy for achieving it. It is important that we define our goal both clearly and precisely from the outset. In this way a goal becomes something that we "really" want rather than just something that we think we "might" want.

It is also important that we consider all the possible ways in which we might achieve our goal, the relative strengths and weaknesses of each approach, and the resources that we might need in order to make our dream a reality. In this way, we should aim to make our goal SMARTER by following the established guidelines for goal setting, and by using such things as the GROW Model to help clarify the process.

Take action: Whilst defining the goal and determining the strategy are important, taking action is absolutely essential. Without action a dream or an aspiration remains exactly that – a dream or an aspiration. Having identified what it is that we want and how we are going to get it, we can only make it a reality by committing to both our goal and our strategy.

In taking action, however, it is important to remember that there are two components to any action – quality and quantity – such that good results are more often a product of people taking the right action (quality) rather than simply taking lots of actions (quantity). In this way, results are usually a function of people working smarter as opposed to harder. Consistency is also important because results are more often than not a product of small, consistent actions taken over a prolonged period of time, rather than something quickly come by.

Find out what works and what doesn't: Whilst some of our actions might improve our performance immediately and place us one step closer to achieving our goal, others may not have the result that we hope for. Finding out what works and what doesn't work is important if we are to preserve the quality of what we are doing and achieve our goal in the shortest period of time.

Having determined a strategy for achieving our goal does not mean that we must follow it doggedly. Goal setting is a dynamic process such that we must be flexible in our approach and be prepared to learn from it at every opportunity. If we are not getting the results that we want from our actions, we must be prepared to change our strategy until we get the results that we do.

All too often people are unhappy with the results that they are getting but continue to do exactly the same things that they have always done – and yet still complain about the (lack of) results they are getting.

Take more action: Having changed our strategy it is essential that we continue to take action. Once again, we may need to consider the quality, quantity and consistency of our actions, and their order and sequence, to ensure we are working SMARTER as opposed to harder. And once again, it is very much a matter of finding out what works and what doesn't work.

Persevere: Assuming that we have followed the process of goal setting properly – that we have defined our goal and determined our strategy, taken action, found out what works and what doesn't work, and taken more action – achieving our goals invariably becomes a question of perseverance. Many people get disillusioned by the fact that their goals can sometimes take a long time to achieve – they want results immediately.

Perhaps we should reflect upon the adage that "most things easily come by are invariably not worth having", and "if it's worth having at all it's (usually) worth waiting for". This is particularly true if we are new to the goal setting process.

Having developed an action plan they should immediately place a "start" and "achievement" date on the goals and use this time scale to monitor progress. This is important in long term career planning and management of expectations. It also means individuals can alter the goal or plan accordingly especially if they are seeing results quicker than anticipated.

The Coaching Skills

Now that I understood and developed a process, there were a set of skills that are commonly used within coaching. These skills are the common skills used, and terminology may change, but in essence they are recognized within the coaching world, but not confined to. They are as follows:

Effective Questions: The primary coaching skill that is used in order to raise awareness during step one and two of the coaching process is the use of effective questioning. In order to question effectively, in coaching the individual must employ a wide variety of questions and questioning techniques – including open and closed, broad and narrow, rhetorical and hypothetical, leading and interrogative, 50/50, and scale of 1-to-10 questions.

In order for these questions to be effective they must raise awareness and generate responsibility. It's at this stage that I began to practice my own effective question techniques. I practiced them everywhere, whether it was grabbing a coffee, doing the shopping or even speaking to my family. I notice that when I got it completely wrong there was that 'dazed' expression on an individual's face: the feedback is instant.

The more results and positive ones that I got, the more I developed a bank of questions that I could use and I could quickly formulate a question to the response that I got from individuals. For this reason, having the ability to ask effective questions is not only important in a coaching context, but can be used as effectively anywhere. Examples of coaching questions that I would use are:

What do you want to achieve?
What is important to you right now?
What would you like to get from the next 30 minutes?
What areas do you want to work on?
Describe your perfect world
What do you want to achieve as a result of this session?

Where are you now in relation to your goal?
On a scale of 1 -10 where are you?
What has contributed to your success so far?
What skills/knowledge/attributes do you have?
What progress have you made so far?
What is working well right now?

What are your options?
How have you tackled this/or had similar situation before?
What could you do differently?
Who do you know who has encountered a similar situation?
If anything was possible what would you do?
What else?

Which options work best for you?
What one small step are you going to take now?
What actions will you take?
When are you going to start?
Who will help you?
How will you know you have been successful?
How will you ensure that you do it?
On a scale of 1 -10 how committed /motivated are you to doing it?

Active Listening: The second skill employed in order to generate responsibility and raise awareness within the coaching process is active listening. In order to actively listen, an individual must first be silent, and then actively engage in the listening process as opposed to passively doing so. This is achieved by a process of "whole body" listening – employing the ears, the eyes, and the heart, in order to make sensory judgments about the person's levels of confidence and motivation.

This is certainly easier said than done. Have you ever been listening to someone's response to a question that you have asked, and you know the answer, yet they still haven't got it, your whole body just wants to scream out the answer! This skill, once you start to pick up on the small things, becomes easy to pick up the more you use, but it takes practice.

An example of this was I had to give an employee some good news that they were promoted, but the promotion would involve moving to a new part of the country. I explained to them that they were being promoted and that it would involve a move and asked the question "are you happy with that?" The response I got was "yes I am happy", but they were shaking their head at the same time, so they were telling me what I wanted to hear, but subconsciously they were telling me something different.

I questioned them on this and found out that they had children in a great school and had just bought a house, so although they wanted the promotion, the move away would be the worse decision at the present time for them given their personal circumstances.

Empathic Responding: When it comes to getting the performance, the skill used in order to facilitate performance during the process is empathic responding. Responding with empathy requires that an individual should have a true understanding of the person's needs before choosing the best response to them.

When responding with empathy it's important to give constructive feedback that builds, and it is always done constructively, even if the result is negative. This seems to go against the grain, and if you think about a time when you got a negative result and you got feedback, traditionally it is done using a transactional style, 'you didn't do this', 'you didn't do that', 'you should have done this', and so on, instead of building and using constructive feedback.

The use of validated praise is used, the validated the "reason why" , how many times have you completed a task and all you get is a well done or good job or words similar. By validating the reason, then you are showing that the reason was understood, for example: "that was a great result because I noticed this", and "you did this".

Otherwise it goes in one ear and out the other. How many times have you witnessed this at work, at home, at school or even with our own children, that when speaking at them they take no responsibility for their subsequent actions.

Chapter 5 – Emotional Intelligence

What Are Emotions?

In order to first understand emotional intelligence, we need to understand what is an emotion is. The scientific answer to that would be that an emotional is a psychological state that has three different components: the subjective experience, a physical response, and a behavioural or expressive response. There are many different ways psychologists have tried to come up with in order to explain emotions.

In 1972, a psychologist by the name of Paul Eckman proposed there are six, basic human emotions that are universal. Those emotions include disgust, fear, anger, happiness, surprise and sadness. In 1999, he expanded that list to include excitement, embarrassment, shame, contempt, pride, amusement, and satisfaction.

In between Eckman's times, in the 1980's, Robert Plutchik suggested another classification system. This system was called the wheel of emotions. He suggested there are different emotions that can be combined with one another in order to create another emotion, just like an artist might mix together the primary colours to make another colour. Plutchik proposes there are eight primary emotions: happiness, sadness, anger, fear, trust, disgust, surprise, and anticipation. When they are combined, they create another emotion. For example, when happiness and anticipation are combined, they may make excitement. So what about the three different components of emotions? This may better help you understand your own.

Subjective Experience

Emotions are subjective even though all humans experience the basic, universal emotions. Regardless of our backgrounds or our cultures, we all experience the same basic emotions such as anger, sadness, or happiness. However, our experience of these emotions is actually unique. For example, not all anger is the same. There are subcategories of anger such as mild annoyance all the way up to blinding range.

We never seem to experience a pure form of each emotion, either. Mixed emotions over an even tor a situation your life is not uncommon. Those who are faced with a new job might feel both excited and nervous. Those who are having children or getting married might have anything from joy to anxiety, to all the emotions in between. They can happen at the same time or they may happen one after the other.

Physical Response

You've most likely felt your stomach lurch or twist when you're anxious or your heart palpate with fear. This is a physical response to your emotions. Many of these responses can include sweaty palms, a racing heart, and rapid breathing. These are all part of the sympathetic nervous system, which a branch of the autonomic nervous system. This part of your nervous system controls the body's fight or flight response, and when faced with a threat, these responses prepare your body to flee or face a threat.

Early studies of the physical forms of emotion focused on autonomic response, recent research has targeted the brain's role in your emotions. Brain scans show that the amygdala, a part of your limbic system, has a role in your emotions, especially fear. This is a tiny, almond shaped component of the brain that has been linked to hunger and thirst, as well as emotion and memory.

Behavioural Response

This final component is most likely the one you are most familiar with, the expression of emotions. We spend a lot of time interpreting emotional expressions of those around us, and our ability to accurately understand the expressions of their emotions is what gives us emotional intelligence. These expressions play a large role in our body language.

Expressions such as smiling or frowning are universal across the globe. Our culture also plays a large role in how we express emotions. For example, in Japan, those who are in the presence of an authority figure mask their fear or disgust. They almost seem to shut-down.

Emotions Allow Us to Understand Others

The emotional expression of others around us provides us with a wealth of social information. Communicating socially is an imperative part of our daily lives and relationships, and when we can interpret and intact with those emotions of others, we're able to build stronger relationships. It allows us to respond in a deeper, more meaningful way that helps us strengthen the bonds with one another. Darwin was one of the earliest researchers who scientifically studied emotions.

He suggested that they are displayed in order for our survival and safety. For example, coming across a hissing or spitting animal tells you the animal is angry and upset. You are more likely to stay away and survive by not getting injured. In addition, we need to be aware of each other's emotions in order to stay out of stressful, dangerous situations and learn how to defuse them successfully.

Emotional Quotient (EQ) & Intelligence Quotient (IQ)

We often refer to how intelligent we are by measuring our IQ, this is a familiar term for most of us. We can also apply this to our knowledge and skills and broadly place them as a representative of a person's IQ. However, linked to our knowledge and skills is our motivation, another way of looking at motivation is our attitude, which is broadly representative of a person's EQ.

Whereas IQ encompasses the verbal, logical-mathematical and visual-spatial intelligences typically taught formally at school through the process of education, EQ comprises the intra-personal and inter-personal intelligences typically learned informally through life experience and the process of socialization. This development of EQ has been led by the likes of Daniel Goleman and is now the subject of development programs in this field alone.

If you have a high EQ, then you're able to see your emotional state, as well as the emotional state of those around you, and draw them to you rather than push them away. You can use your understanding of their emotions in order to relate to them better, and form healthier relationships.

Goleman suggests, that our EQ is made up of the following: Self Awareness, Self-Regulation, Motivation, Empathy and Social Skills. It's worth expanding on these, because once I understood what they meant I was able to better understand other people and how their respective EQ can be developed. This EQ could also be place into an organization and therefore has a role within the VBL Model:

Self-Awareness: The ability to understand your strengths and own weaknesses, your internal motivations, drives and preferences, and how you appear to both yourself and other people. Basically understanding who you are.

Self-Regulation: Based upon your own self-awareness, the ability to appropriately control the emotions that drive your behaviour in different situations, and if you think before you act. This is basically knowing right from wrong. It is ok to think it, but you know to act upon it is wrong.

Motivation: Based upon self-regulation, the ability to direct your internal resources, your knowledge, skills and attitudes, towards a predetermined outcome or goal. This can be internal and external depending on the situation or goal that needs to be achieved.

Empathy: Based upon motivation, the ability to understand the strengths and weakness of other people, their internal motivations, drives and preferences, and consider their needs and viewpoints. The way I look at this is walking in someone else's shoes but keeping your own socks on. Not to be confused with sympathy.

Social Skills: Based upon empathy, the ability to establish, maintain and develop relationships and communicate effectively to get what you want whilst respecting the rights of other people. This is the part that others see when looking at your EQ.

Why is EQ so Important?

EQ is very important for everyone. We know that individuals who are the smartest are not always the most successful, or the most fulfilled in their lives. We can probably recall someone who is academically brilliant, but they are not socially graceful, and unsuccessful in their work, or their personal relationships due to their ineptness.

Our intellectual intelligence is not enough for us to be successful and happy in life. Your IQ can get you into university, but your EQ is what will help you manage your emotions, and stress, when your facing exams.

Your EQ affects your work life significantly. If you have a high EQ, you can navigate the social complexities of your workplace, and lead or motivate others. You can excel in your chosen career. When it comes to gauging job candidates as an example, companies view EQ as more important than technical ability.

Developing my own EQ has helped me within all forms employment as a consultant and in general life, and therefore plays a part within coaching.

Developing Emotional Intelligence

Do you have emotional intelligence? The truth is that everyone has some level of what is referred to as emotional intelligence – some people just have more of it than others. If you are lacking emotional intelligence, luckily you can learn to develop more of it and use it in your everyday life. But first, how do you know whether you have a lot of emotional intelligence, or only a little? In order to answer this, you will first have to understand what emotional intelligence is.

Emotional intelligence is all about being able to know what people around you are feeling – what their emotions are. People with high emotional intelligence can easily tell what people they are associating with are feeling, and can then use it to benefit both themselves and others. If you understand what others are feeling, you will know how to treat them, talk to them, successfully work with them, and so much more.

You are probably wondering how you can develop your emotional intelligence. Well, you need to try to be more aware of your surroundings. Next time you are around others, try to take in all the little things about them that can signify what they are feeling. Are you someone who is generally caught up in a million things at once? Are you often stressed, worried, and frazzled? If this sounds like you, then you might be having trouble developing emotional intelligence because you don't take the time to focus on what is going

To develop your emotional intelligence, try practicing mindfulness. Mindfulness is just focusing on the present – instead of what might happen in the future or what has happened in the past. It sounds so simple, doesn't it? However, the truth is that with all the distractions of life, putting it into practice can be another story entirely.

Chapter 6 – GROW Tool

History

The GROW Tool is a simple method for goal It was developed in the United Kingdom and was used extensively in corporate coaching in the late 1980s and 1990s. There have been many claims to authorship of GROW as a way of achieving goals and solving problems.

While no one person can be clearly identified as the originator, Sir John Whitmore has made significant contributions. The GROW tool was influenced by the Inner Game method developed by Timothy Gallwey. Gallwey was a tennis coach who noticed that he could often see what a player was doing incorrectly but that simply telling him/her what he/she should be doing did not bring about lasting change.

The parallel between Gallwey's Inner Game method and the GROW tool method, can be illustrated by the example of a player who does not keep his or her eye on the ball. Some coaches might give instructions such as: 'Keep your eye on the ball' to try to correct this. The problem with this sort of instruction is that a player will be able to follow it for a short while but may be unable to keep it in the front of his or her mind in the long term. So one day, instead of giving an instruction, Gallwey asked the player to say 'bounce' out loud when the ball bounced and 'hit' out loud when she hit it.

The result was that the players started to improve without a lot of effort because they were keeping their eye on the ball. But because of the way the instruction was given they did not have a voice in their heads saying 'I must keep my eye on the ball.' Instead they were playing a simple game while they were playing tennis. Once Gallwey saw how play could be improved in this way, he stopped giving instructions and started asking questions that would help the player discover for herself what worked and what needed to change. This was the birth of the Inner Game method.

The GROW tool is similar. For example, the first stage in this process would be to set a target which the player wants to achieve. If a player wanted to improve his/her first serve Gallwey would ask how many first serves out of ten, would he/she like to get in. This is the *Goal*. The *Reality* would be defined by asking the player to serve 10 balls and seeing how many first serves went in.

Gallwey would then ask awareness-raising questions such as 'What do you notice you are doing differently when the ball goes in or out?' This would enable the player to discover for themselves, what was changing about their mind and body when the serve went in or out. He/She had then defined her *Obstacles* and *Options*. He/She therefore learned for themselves what they had to change in order to meet their serving targets and they had a clear *Will* – what they will do.

The originators of both the Inner Game method and the GROW Tool suggested that many individuals were struggling to achieve goals because they were not learning from experience and were not aware of the available knowledge that would help them.

It's worth noting that Sir John Whitmore and Tim Gallwey would often work together, hence why I take the position of Sir John being the most responsible for the implementation of the GROW Tool.

The GROW Tool

Having established, the coaching process and skills, it is important to have a deep understanding of the tools that could be used within coaching. Whilst the GROW Tool is most commonly used in the context of one-on-one coaching, it can be employed in the context of personal goal setting and workplace goal setting too. The GROW tool is essentially a framework for directing effective questions about the goal and its achievement. It can be used in conjunction with other coaching and management tools. It consists of four stages:

Goal: This stage involves us focusing our attention solely on the outcome or performance goal that we ultimately desire. Here it is important that we employ all the tools and guidelines applicable to goals and the goal setting process. The outcome of this stage should be a goal that is both clearly and precisely defined – accepting of course that it may well change in the future.

The type of questions we might ask ourselves at this stage could include "what do I want to achieve", "how might I make this goal more specific", "how can I make this goal measurable" and "do I really think that my goal is achievable by me through my own efforts"? We might also ask ourselves, "are there any sub-goals that I might include as milestones to reaching my goal" and "when do I want to have achieved my goal by"?

In order to get the right goal we have to employ SMART. I have seen too often goals that are not set using SMART and ultimately they fail. This is true of company objectives, if they are not set using SMART then ultimately the company has little chance of achieving them.

Reality: This stage involves us considering our current situation by reflecting upon where we are "now" in relation to our goal. The most important criterion for doing this is objectivity. Often people distort their reality with the opinions, judgments, expectations and beliefs of other people – in addition to those that they undoubtedly hold themselves.

For this reason it is important for us to maintain a degree of detachment and be descriptive rather than evaluative. At the end of this stage it is usually worth checking that the original goal that we made is still valid. Many people find that they need to amend it in light of what they have learned about themselves during the reality stage.

The type of questions we might ask ourselves at this stage could include, "what is my current situation now with respect to my goal", "how close to my goal am I", "what are the reasons for this" and "how do I think achieving my goal will make me think, feel and act in the future"? In terms of our graduate, the reality could be what is your current position in relation to being the CEO? What is your current score in relation to achieving your KPI score for the year?

Options: Having looked at the reality of our current situation, this stage involves us considering the options available in terms of how we might make our goal a reality. It is important to recognize, however, that the purpose of this stage is not so much to find the "right" answer, as it is to create and list as many alternatives as possible.

In doing so, we should continually try to think "outside of the box", whilst reflecting objectively on the relative strengths and weakness of each option, what things we might already have in support of each option, and yet other things we might need. Throughout this stage we have to beware of negative assumptions such as "that option wouldn't work" or "I wouldn't be allowed to do that".

By asking ourselves effective questions, or better still getting other people to ask them of us, we can over-ride this negative and self-limiting tendency and challenge the reality of our situation by asking ourselves "what are the reasons for me thinking this way". Similarly, the "what if" approach often produces yet more options. In this way we might ask ourselves, "what if I had more time" or "what if this wasn't the case". Often, however, we might be unable to see an option that someone else can.

Here, we might ask others, "are there any options that I haven't yet considered?" But having asked the question we must at least be prepared to consider the answer! Examples of other questions that we might ask during this stage might include "how might I achieve this goal", "how have other people achieved similar goals" and "what other options might I have open to me"? This ends up a list of action points on what you could do, it's not the list of what you will do although it is easy to mix the two up.

Will: Whilst the Options stage is about what we "could" do, the Will stage is about what we "will" do. This is arguably the most important stage because it is the one in which decisions are made and from which action is derived. It is during this stage that we ask ourselves "what option(s) will I choose?"

Having run down our list of options and summarized them, we may well have just one preferred option that we wish to act upon or several that we wish to implement at once. Alternatively, we might prioritize several options on the basis of "if that doesn't work then I'll do this". Once we have made our choice, it is often a good idea to check that our chosen course of action will help us achieve our goal.

It is then essential to commit to our time scale by asking ourselves, "when will I start working towards my goal?" If we have employed the GROW tool properly, committing to our action plan in this way is the natural conclusion to the goal setting process.

I have seen this tool adapted by other consultants, authors and coaches, especially if they are creating their own coaching tools and change the "will" to "way forward". This would be my only gripe on this, as normally the words change but the meaning stays the same, but in the 'way forward' it ends up 'wishy washy', you have just created a really SMART Goal and then right at the end the action plan is not as specific as it could be, if the word 'will' is used.

Going back to the example questions that I mentioned earlier in this chapter, I can now place them into examples of GROW Tool questions as follows:

Goal Questions:

What do you want to achieve?
What is important to you right now?
What would you like to get from the next 30 minutes?
What areas do you want to work on?
Describe your perfect world
What do you want to achieve as a result of this session?

Reality Questions:

Where are you now in relation to your goal?
On a scale of 1 -10 where are you?
What has contributed to your success so far?
What skills/knowledge/attributes do you have?
What progress have you made so far?
What is working well right now?

Option Questions:

What are your options?
How have you tackled this/or had similar situation before?
What could you do differently?
Who do you know who has encountered a similar situation?
If anything was possible what would you do?
What else?

Will Questions:

Which options work best for you?
What one small step are you going to take now?
What actions will you take?
When are you going to start?
Who will help you?
How will you know you have been successful?
How will you ensure that you do it?
On a scale of 1 -10 how committed /motivated are you to doing it?

A friend of mine wrote a technical book on training management[9] and they incorporated this tool into a number of elements within the system that they had created, which proves that it can be adapted and used outside of the context of coaching. It can be used as easily in other forms of business and management to illicit results. This is an example of why GROW has ended up being labelled the primary coaching tool.

Motivation

---

[9] Cording, Vincent E, (2014), *Training Management – The Six Stage Training Model,* Amazon

It would be no good if an individual's motivation was lacking or they were ill equipped to motivate themselves. Motivation is the driving force behind burning ambition, determination and commitment. It is also one of the most difficult areas of psychology to understand.

Most psychological theories concentrate on either the personal or situational factors that account for differences in motivation. But there are fundamental principles that invariably hold true, irrespective of the other ways in which we might consider motivation, that provide powerful insights into why people do the things they do and why, and sometimes, they don't do the things that perhaps they know they should.

Getting them to be highly motivated was key, and the secret to attaining motivation is by the use of goal setting, and going through the process explained earlier. If this is in place then they have to be motivated to get the results. You cannot progress to a performance stage if they haven't generated the responsibility. This reinforces the fact that you cannot move onto the next stage without the prior one in place.

Attitude

All of the above had to be linked with a person's attitude, they have to have the right one don't they? On a day-to-day basis, people and organizations enter situations, meet people and encounter things that have the potential to impact upon our attitude, with both positive and negative. An understanding of attitude is therefore important because how we think determines how we feel, how we feel determines what we do, and what we do ultimately determines our performance.

In this way, attitude is central to such things as optimism and a person's state of mind. It is therefore important to maintain a positive mental attitude in order to maximize performance, which you can see links back to the definition of coaching that we discussed earlier. It has to be linked to get the performance.

By being around positive people, watching motivational programs and reading positive books, whether they be personal development texts, or inspirational biographies or simply good novels, it is possible to acquire a positive attitude through vicarious or social learning.

By identifying these things and subjecting ourselves to them on a regular basis we can condition ourselves accordingly. We can learn, adopt and become positive people or organizations, and the more positive we are the more we are likely to achieve positive results.

Practical Exercise

Now that I have explained in essence the "what and how" of coaching, as a leadership tool within VBL, let's try a little practice. For this you will need a piece of paper, pen or pencil, A4 size will be the most suitable for this. I will refer back to this exercise later in the book.

I want you to draw a large rectangle to the left side of the piece of paper but leave a big enough gap on the right side so that you can place in some notes. At the top of the paper, towards the left and above the rectangle, I want you to write the word Goal.

Now that we have this in place I want you to think of a specific career goal that you want to achieve: it could be an appointment, or something as achieving a particular KPI at work. I want you then to apply SMART to the goal that you have written. Does it stand up to applying SMART? If it does then great, if not, you need to change the Goal so that you can achieve the SMART principles.

At the bottom left below the rectangle I want you to write Reality, and place in where you are now in relation to the goal that you have written. For example, if the goal was an appointment or promotion the reality could be your present position, if it was a KPI, the reality could be the KPI current score in relation to the score that you want to achieve (Goal).

You now have the "where you want to be", and the "where you are". Now place on the right towards the top the word Options, and I want you to produce a list of everything that you could do in order to achieve the goal, there is no right or wrong for this, but just keep writing everything that you can think of to achieve the goal.

Now that you have your options written down I want you to analyze what you have written down and pick one the you Will do, one point from the list that you have written down and that you Will do. I am going to hold you to this, that your committing to do that one thing.

If you then look at the rectangle that you have drawn, you could place on that one task that you will do in the form of a step, and once you have completed that step you have moved closer towards achieving that goal. Imagine you had produced all the steps required and achieved them, then you would have achieved the goal.

Below is representation of the GROW Tool:

GROW Tool

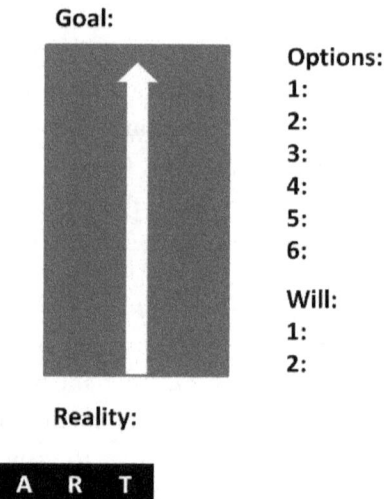

Goal:

Options:
1:
2:
3:
4:
5:
6:

Will:
1:
2:

Reality:

S M A R T

Chapter 7 – The Wheel of Life

Many people set out to become peak performers without really knowing why they want to do so. The Wheel of Life is a useful tool with which to consider performance as it relates to life as a whole. It allows people to reflect upon the things that really matter in life and keep them balanced and in proper perspective.

For these reasons, it is a useful tool to employ immediately prior to goal setting or in order to confirm the purpose and validity of performance interventions.

Analogy

The Wheel of Life is in essence an analogy. It takes the view that life "rolls on and on", much like a wheel, from the day we are born until the day that we pass away. And whilst we might not be able to control when our life starts, or indeed when it stops, we can take responsibility for and control the direction our life takes and the quality of the ride.

The analogy suggests that in order for a smooth or quality ride, a person's wheel must have balanced spokes for it to run strong and true.

The analogy is useful because it suggests that our dreams, goals and aspirations must be balanced if we are to keep things in proper perspective. In doing so, it provides an alternative view of performance that emphasises happiness, fulfilment and growth, rather than just success and achievement.

Method

The Wheel of Life is usually generated immediately prior to goal setting, in conjunction with Empowering Questions, or whilst goal setting in order to confirm the purpose and validity of performance interventions. It is usually generated in four stages as follows:

1.   Identify the areas of life that are most important and integrate them within a Wheel of Life.

2.   On a scale of 1 to 10, rate the current level of performance in these areas in terms of happiness, fulfilment and growth.

3.   Assess which areas offer the greatest opportunity for happiness, fulfilment and growth by considering profile

discrepancies.

4.   Assess the extent to which all of these things are balanced and in proper perspective.

The Wheel of Life

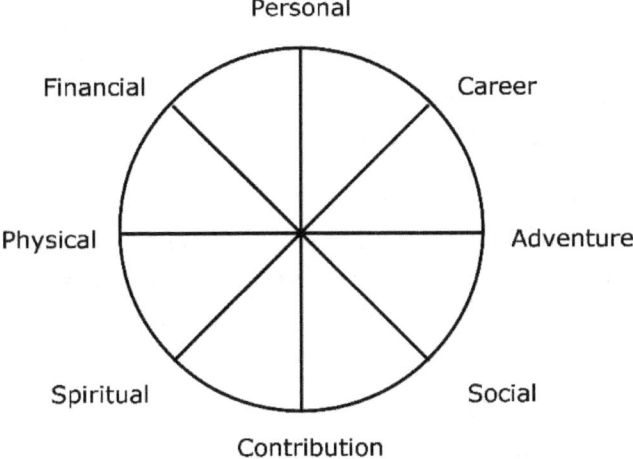

The Spokes

Whilst any Wheel of Life should necessarily be labelled by the person generating it, a basic application would probably label the spokes of a wheel as follows:

Personal: The area of our life concerned with our

development as an individual and our overall desire to improve our performance and achieve more. Many people see this area as relating to their cognitive and self-actualisation needs.

In terms of furthering our knowledge and understanding of themselves and the world in which we live and becoming everything that we might want to be and are capable of becoming.

It could just as easily relate to our hobbies and interests, however, and any number of other things that might give us a personal sense of satisfaction. In this way, we might have personal goals to learn to speak a foreign language or play a musical instrument.

Career: The area of our life most obviously concerned with the goals we have about our employment or profession. It invariably relates to our physical and safety needs in terms of providing for both self and family and usually includes aspirations of advancement and promotion.

But could just as easily be performance related in terms of "being the best that we can be". Consequently, it will often include education and personal development goals in addition to those purely professional.

Adventure: This area of our life is a usually the natural extension of our personal and social goals. It might therefore include any goals we might have to travel and all those hobbies, interests and activities that we really like doing, or might really like to take up if money and time were no object.

It might include swimming with dolphins, sky diving, climbing the Matterhorn, visiting Peru – or anything else that takes our fancy.

Social: The area of our life concerned with relationships and how we feel about other people. As such, it most obviously relates to our social needs in terms of love and belonging.

Our goals in this area would usually involve us improving the quality of our relationships with family and friends, but could just as easily extend to a love of community, humanity and even any naturalistic interests that we might also have.

Contribution: This area of our life is often the most compelling because it provides an opportunity for us to leave "our mark", "create a legacy", or make a true difference to other people.

Whilst we may aim for a project as grand as setting up a charity or foundation that offers opportunities to disadvantaged people, we might be content with something as simple as committing to our local youth club or spending more time with our family.

Spiritual: This area of our life is often the least explored. In many ways, however, it offers the greatest potential for happiness, fulfilment and growth. Our goals in this area need not necessarily relate to any particular religion, however, or be specifically spiritual in and of themselves – we might just as easily define them as being philosophical instead.

Irrespective, this area relates to us reflecting upon the "bigger questions" in life in order to "be at one" with ourselves and our existence.

Physical: The area of our life concerned with our physical body and issues of health and vitality. Most people will see this area as relating to fitness, optimum nutrition and following a healthy lifestyle – accepting of course that we all have different interpretations as to what health and fitness actually mean and the extent to which they are important.

Without doubt, most of us have very specific and personal goals relating to this area. And so we perhaps should because, in a very real sense, the body is the "vehicle" in which we travel through life!

Financial: The area of our life concerned with money, wealth and material possessions. Whilst many people have an in-built fear of being seen as overly materialistic, we should nevertheless recognise that hard earned possessions can give a lot of satisfaction and a certain sense of achievement.

In the modern world, meanwhile, money is invariably a necessity for us to satisfy those other needs that we invariably have, and allow us to provide for both ourselves and our families. Consequently, we should never be ashamed of having financial or material goals, although it is probably important to keep these things in proper perspective.

Labelling Spokes

In accepting that life is not just about goals, but also about roles, some people prefer to label the Wheel of Life in this way. Consequently, we might, for example, re-label the social area of our life Son, Husband or Father, and the professional area of our life Manager or Salesperson accordingly.

The spokes mentioned can be changed by the coach to suit the need of the coachee, the ones mentioned are just shown as an illustration of what could be used.

Application

Many people set out to achieve specific goals, in their respective lives, without really knowing why they want to do so. The Wheel of Life is a useful tool with which to consider performance as it relates to life as a whole.

It allows people to reflect upon the things that really matter in life and keep them balanced and in proper perspective. For these reasons, it is a useful tool to employ immediately prior to goal setting or in order to confirm the purpose and validity of performance interventions.

Example

Using the spokes that were previously mentioned, as an example illicit the responses from the coachee by getting them to identify the areas of life that are most important to and integrate them within the Wheel of Life. On a scale of 1 to 10, get the coachee to rate thier current level of performance in those areas in terms of happiness, fulfilment and growth. Which areas offer the greatest opportunity for happiness, fulfilment and growth by considering profile discrepancies? To what extent are all of these things balanced and in proper perspective?

The coachee should now rate themselves where they want to be and where they would like to be on the scale of 1 – 10. An example how the results could be shown are listed below:

Spokes	Where you want to be	Where you are Now
Personal	9	5
Career	8	6
Adventure	6	5
Social	7	7
Contribution	5	5
Spiritual	4	4
Physical	8	6
Financial	8	5

Using the scores that the coachee has provided for each spoke of the wheel of life they can now be plotted onto a wheel of life representation. In this example the biggest gap identified is in the personal spoke. The coachee in the example has suggested that they would like to be a 9, but currently they are scoring a 5. Below is the example wheel of life representation:

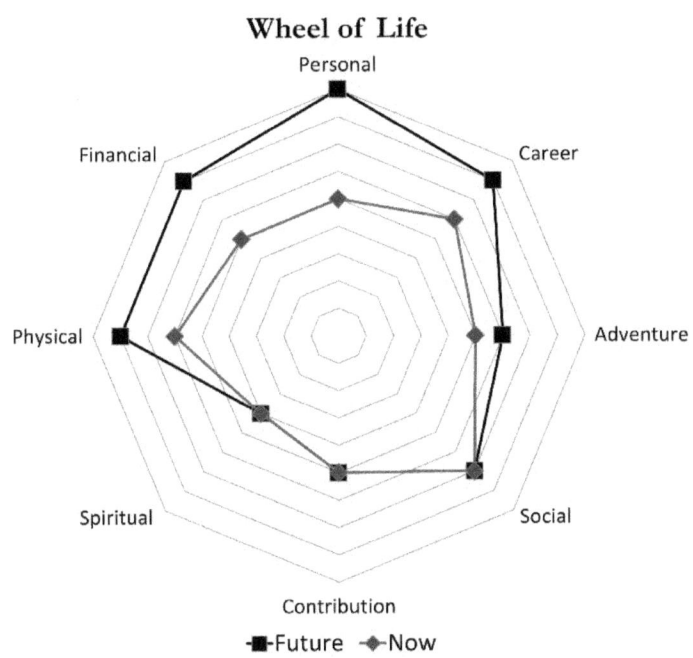

Wheel of Life

M A. Grant

Chapter 8 – Examples

Putting it all Together

How do we then use this information gleamed from the wheel of life, that we used as an example in the previous chapter? If we look at the chart that was created, we need to establish the performance gaps from the chart and/or wheel that was constructed.

Looking at the spokes from this example, then the biggest performance gap is related to the personal spoke. In this particular spoke, on the wheel, the score that was wanted was a score of 9, the score of where we are in relation to this was a score of 5. In performance terms we now have a gap of 4 to close in order to drive towards achieving the goal of 9.

Using the wheel of life is a great way to gather information, but as a coach we now need to turn that data into practical application. It's great to have the data, but what do we do with it? What does coaching look like from here on?

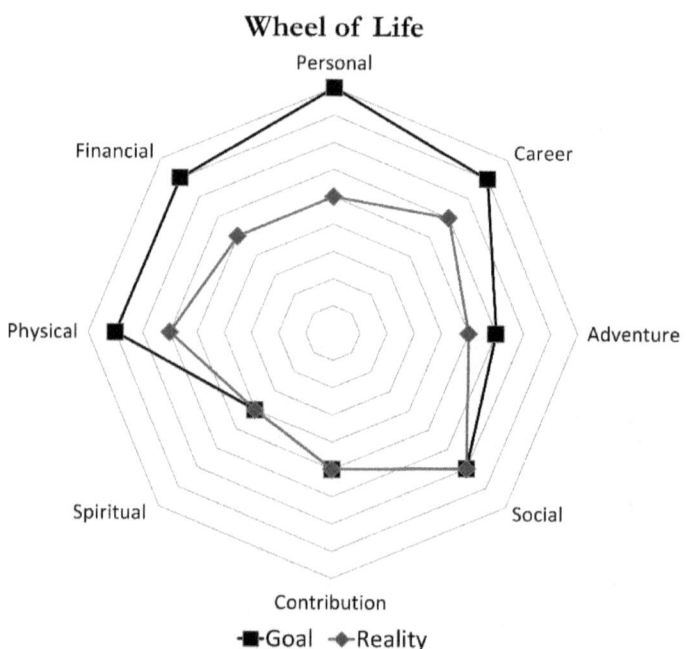

Wheel of Life

Practical Application

Once we have the information, we can present this information back to the coachee in the form of the above mentioned diagram. This is great for the coachee as it represents a visual representation, which helps stimulate the desire to change.

Using the primary coaching tool the GROW we can now move on to combine the wheel of life, moving from a 5, to a 9, within the "personal" spoke. Explaining to the coachee that we are going to use the GROW tool to help achieve that specific goal. The goal now changes to the where you want to be from the wheel of life, in this case we can place on the 9. The reality at the bottom of the GROW tool, become the where are you from the wheel of life, the 5.

Using the Options and Will stage as previously shown, the coachee now has a GROW Tool superseded onto the performance gap from the wheel of life as shown below:

Linked to Wheel of Life

Goal: Score 9

Reality: Score 5

S M A R T

Options:
1. List every thing that you could do to raise your score from a 5 to 9.
2. Brainstorm everything that you can think of. The more you could do, the better.

Will:
1. Produce a detailed action plan to drive from a 5 to a 9.

Coaching Models

There is an extreme amount of coaching models, like the wheel of life, that are available to coaches to use. As coaches develop their skills, and gain results with coaches, then they can get a feel for what coaching models work for them.

Exploring the different types of models that are out there would be the excuse for a whole new book. But if you think about what I have shown you in the wheel of life, and then placing the GROW tool on top of the performance gap, this is what a coach is going to reproduce for each coaching session.

In order to close a performance gap once one has been identified then the primary tool, the GROW is going to be adopted. This can be used and adapted not only from a purely coaching perspective, but overlapped in the work place.

Imagine now that you are conducting a performance appraisal preview at the beginning of the year, using KPIs as the performance component. Discussing this with the employee, you will end up with the KPI score to be achieved for the year, and the current score.

If you now use the GROW tool. The desired KPI score becomes the GOAL, and the current KPI score the Reality. The employee now takes on the responsibility of achieving the score, with the employer taking on the role of coach in this example.

For the employer this is a "win win" as if the employee

achieves the KPI, it will have a performance implication for the business, and ultimately the bottom line. But because the employee takes responsible for their results then, if the employee does not achieve them, this allows the employer to take a much more transactional stance. It moves this from a "soft skill" to a more robust one. It becomes an enabler.

The thing here is to discover how this application can work for you, what works best for you to get the desired results with the coachee.

M A. Grant

Chapter 9 – The Secret

Why Change

Before I reveal the secret of coaching, it is important to realise, why would we want to change? Irrespective of the way in which we might want to improve our performance, achieve more and realise our true potential, the process that underpins all of these things is the process of change. Unfortunately, the very nature of change makes most people feel extremely uncomfortable such that they are often resistant to it.

We can consider the process of change, in terms of the different stages that people typically pass through in order to change, the difference between transactional and transformational change, and the barriers that most often prevent them from doing so. An understanding of these, enables us to better guide and facilitate the process of change, adhere to any action plan or programme we might choose to embark on, and subsequently get the type of result that we want.

Physical Discomfort. This acknowledges that simply embarking on the process of change is for most people somewhat uncomfortable. In this way, the stage can be considered a barrier and represents our first exit point from the process of change.

Physical Reward. If we are able to deal with this physical discomfort, and adhere to the action plan or programme we have embarked upon, we enter the second stage. This stage acknowledges the extrinsic benefits we might receive by the accomplishment of any short-term outcome or goal. Having perhaps achieved the result that we wanted, however, also represents a possible exit point from the process of change.

Transformational Change. This type of change that is realised between these two stages is often referred to as "transactional" change. This term describes change that is realised at the level of actions and results. "Transformational" change, meanwhile, describes change that is realised at the level of self-image and beliefs such that it is the person, as opposed to their behaviour, that is fundamentally changed such that the person is considered "transformed".

Transactional v Transformational Change

This type of change can only be realised if we adhere to our action plan or programme through to the final stage, that of Psychological Reward.

This stage acknowledges the intrinsic benefits we might receive by the accomplishment of any long-term outcome or goal. This is at the stage at which our behaviours have been fully integrated, such that they are a fundamental part of who we are as opposed to just something that we do. It is this transformation that results in the adherence to the process of change long after the physical rewards have been realised.

THE STAGES OF CHANGE

The Stages of Change Model considers the six distinct stages that a person must necessarily pass through in order to experience long-term, transformational change. The stages of change are described in terms of:

Pre-Contemplation. During this stage of the process we are "not thinking about change". This could be due to a general lack of awareness or possibly mean that we are in denial. It is usually an external trigger (someone or something) rather than self-contemplation that results in a shift of awareness.

Contemplation. During this stage of the process we are "thinking about change". It is at this stage that we might start to consider the general way in which we might want to change and the benefits and consequences of doing so.

Preparation. During this stage of the process we are "preparing to change". It is at this stage that we start to analysis the specific way in which we want to change and the specific process way by which we intend to do so. It is the stage during which the setting of a clearly and precisely defined goal and a dedicated action plan of how to achieve it is most important.

It is also the stage during which we might develop any additional knowledge and skills, or require any external resources, in order to move to the next stage of change.

Action. During this stage of the process we are "making change". It is at this stage that we must take quality and quantity actions consistent in order to get the result. During this stage, the use of both body-mind and mind-body techniques is useful in order to both generate the Ideal Performance State and maintain a positive attitude.

Relapse / Termination. Relapse and Termination are both stages during which we "stop making changes". Relapse is the stage in which we fail to take quality and quantity actions, adhere to our action plan or programme, thus exit the process of change as a result. Should we enter this stage it is usually necessary to return to the stage of Contemplation in order to re-enter the change process again. Termination, meanwhile, is the stage in which we choose to exit the change process having realised a short-term, transactional result.

Maintenance. Maintenance is the stage in which we "continue to make changes" in order to keep realising a long-term, transformational result. It is the stage during which our effective use of performance interventions starts to become autonomous and habitual.

Change

Irrespective of the way in which we might want to improve our performance, achieve more and realise our true potential, the process that underpins all of these things is the process of change. Unfortunately, the very nature of change makes most people feel extremely uncomfortable such that they are often resistant to it.

In terms of the different stages that people typically pass through in order to change, the difference between transactional and transformational change, and the barriers that most often prevent them from doing so. An understanding of these things enables us to better guide and facilitate the process of change, adhere to any action plan or programme we might choose to embark on, and subsequently get the type of result that we want.

The Journey

Coming to the end of my coaching journey I realise that I have had time to reflect on what went well and the areas that didn't go to well. From the point of view within coaching

Life throws us challenges and asks us to ask those difficult questions, how we answer them is important in all our journeys. I look sometimes at some of the people that I have come across, and look at them now, and they have gone on to have the most fantastic careers, often far surpassing that of mine. It gives me the most reward seeing them realize their potential: isn't it, after all, what we coaches do?

Do we hold people back or do we allow them to grow? This goes with those organizations that I have been fortunate to have worked with.

Challenge

Here is my challenge to you, if you have made it to here, you will have had to have thought about yourself, you will have had to question your own coaching. Therefore I challenge you to go back to the GROW that you did on yourself and reflect, can you make the steps necessary to achieve that particular goal?

The Coaching Secret

The big reveal, the big coaching mystery, by now you will have noticed that it's about simplifying as much as we can in order to get the desired results from coaching. For me it's about not making something it's not, and this is the same for coaching.

It's not magic, there is no dark art to it. People like me, consultants, like to try and make it something special, something only experts can use or do. It's only for those at the top of coaching, those selected individuals. We like to try and keep it that way as it keeps individuals like me in business. Certainly there is a great living to made as a coaching consultant.

Consultants, trainers and training organizations, as an example, don't want to give it away do they? If they do this it will put them out of business. But this goes against the values of true leadership, it can never be about me, it has to be what is important to the individual or organization.

The Ugly Truth

If you haven't turned to this page from the beginning of the book, and you have held back from reading this section, this is the part where after building coaching, taking you on this journey it's time to reveal the big secret of coaching

So here is my big secret to coaching – the ugly truth of coaching that people like me don't want you to know, who are the people like me though? These are all the trainers, coaches, consultants, training companies, consultation companies that are out to make money from you. These are the line managers that are holding you back, the organizational management that don't want to allow growth. The individuals that keep everything to themselves, a little knowledge is power.

This is what they don't want you to know, the ugly truth to coaching is that there is NO SECRET. If you have been paying attention throughout the book you will have been thinking that this makes sense, I could do that, and the truth is you can, of course you can. With a little development and hard work of course you can, I am living proof that yes you can.

You don't need to spend a fortune on expensive programmes that may or may not work, just think about the type of coaching you want to adopt and make it happen yourself. Think about the process we spoke about earlier: what I have been doing is raising your awareness to coaching and generating responsibility in you, the performance is now up to you...

In real terms coaching comes down to your ability to ask an effective question. If you have this ability, you can coach.

References and Reading List

The Point

Normally at the back of the book, tucked away, are the references, which I bet none of you have really read have you? It's true it serves a purpose to support the writing of the book, but what is the point in listing all of them if they serve no real purpose? For me the reading list serves as a "go to" list for anyone interested in taking their underpinning knowledge and developing it further.

This reading list serves as an impartial list of those individuals who have made an impact in coaching and the development of coaching. These offer the current up to date thinking, and some of the most respected individuals in their respective fields.

Throughout the book I have highlighted where applicable those individuals, books and articles I thought would provide an additional source of reading to help the underpinning knowledge. Working within coaching then it also helps to have the academic back up when asked by clients: where does this come from?

Is there any reference we could look to in order to back up what you're saying. Being able to suggest some academic literature is always good when dealing with organizations.

For me, having a library of reference books or knowing where to go to get them is also good, especially when developing new material or looking to give appropriate advice. There is also something rewarding about reading a book or paper.

The list provided is a suggested reading list of some of the books, articles that I have used along the way to enhance my knowledge. They also stand up as points of reference if required. They also point to other directions of investigations too. I am not suggesting to read them all, but have a look through and see if there any that stand out, certainly Whitmore, Goleman, House, Hardy are some individuals that I find personally enjoyable and developmental.

But that is it, they are just a list that I have found useful, they are not the definitive list, just examples of references and books that I have used. Think of my list in the same way that I presented the leadership styles, they are just examples not the examples, use if required but better to have a list and not use it than to want a list of proven leadership material and not have it.

Reading List

Alexander, Graham (2010). "Behavioural coaching the GROW model". In Passmore, Jonathan. *Excellence in coaching: the industry guide* (2nd ed.). London; Philadelphia: Kogan Page. pp. 83–93

Amabile, T.M. (1998). How to kill creativity. *Harvard Business Review, 76(9):* 77-87.

Atwater, L, E. & Yammarino, F, J. (2003). Personal attributes as predictors of superiors and subordinates perceptions of military academy leadership. *Human Relations, 46,* 654 – 668.

Bachkirova, T., & Cox, E. (2004). A bridge over troubled water: bringing together coaching and counselling. *The International Journal of Mentoring and Coaching,* 2.

Baldwin, T, T., Magjuka, R, J., & Loher, B, T. (1991). The perils of participation: effects of choice on training motivation and learning. *Personnel Psychology, 44,* 51–65.

Barling, J., Weber, T., & Kelloway, E, K. (1996). Effects of transformational leadership training on attitudinal and financial outcomes. *Journal of Applied Psychology, 81,* 827-832.

Bass, B.M. (1985). *Leadership and performance beyond expectations.* New York: Free Press.

Bass, B.M., & Avolio, B.J. (1994). *Improving organizational effectiveness through transformational leadership.* Thousand Oaks, CA: Sage.

Bass, B.M., Avolio, B.J., Jung, D., & Berson, Y. (2003).

Predicting unit performance by assessing transformational and transactional leadership. *Journal of Applied Psychology*, 88: 207-218.

Butler, R. (1989). *Psychological Preparation of Olympic Boxers.* In Kremer, J., & Crawford, W., (Eds), *The Psychology of Sport: Theory and Practice (pp74-78).* Leicester: British Psychological Society.

Burns, J. M. (2001). *In a teleconference at the Bernard M Bass Festschrift, State University of New York at Binghampton,* New York, 31 May – 1 June 2001.

Boyer, N. (2003). Leaders mentoring leaders: Unveiling role identity in an international online environment. *Mentoring & Tutoring: Partnership in Learning, 11(1),* 25–42.

Bryman, A., & Bell, W. (2007). *Business Research Methods* (2nd ed). New York. Oxford University Press.

Clutterbuck, D. (2007). *Coaching the Team at Work.* London, Nicholas Brealey.

Cooper, D. R, & Shindler, P. S. (2008). *Business Research Methods* (10th ed). Boston. McGraw-Hill.

Callow, N., Smith, J., Hardy, L., Arthur, C., & Hardy, J. (2009). Measurement of Transformational leadership and its relationship with team cohesion and performance level. *Journal of Applied Sport Psychology, 21 (4),* 395 — 412

Colquitt, J, A., LePine, A., & Noe, R, A. (2000). Toward an integrative theory of training motivation: a meta-analytic path analysis of 20 years of research. *Journal of Applied Psychology, 85* (5), 678–707.

Compton W. C, (2005). An Introduction to Positive Psychology. Thomson Wadsworth.

Cording, Vincent E, (2014), *Training Management – The Six Stage Training Model,* Amazon

Csoka, L. S., & Fiedler, F. E. (1972). The effect of military leadership training: a test of the contingency model. *Organizational Behaviour and Human Performance, 8 (3),* 395–

Dvir, T., Eden, D., Avolio, B. J., & Shamir, B. (2002). Impact of transformational leadership on follower development and performance: a field experiment. *Academy of Management Journal, 45(4),* 735–744.

Ergi, C, P., & Herman, S. (2000). Leadership in the North American environmental Sector: Values, Leadership Styles, and contexts of environmental leaders and their organizations. *Academy of Management Journal, 43,* 571-604.

Ely, K., Boyace, L, A,. Nelson, J, K., Zaccaro, S, J,. Broome, G. & Whyman, W. (2010). Evaluating leadership coaching: A review and integrated framework. *The leadership Quarterly, 21,* 585 – 599.

Festinger, L. (1959). *A Theory of Cognitive Dissonance.* Stanford, CA. Stanford University Press.

Gross, R. (2001). *Psychology: The science of mind and behaviour.* Hodder & Stoughton.

Gallwey, T, W. (1974). *The inner game of tennis.* Random House.

Goleman, D., Boyatzis, R., & Annie McKee. (2002). *The*

new leaders: transforming the art of leadership into the science of results, London: Little, Brown.

Hardy, L., Arthur, C., Jones, G., Shariff, A., Munnoch, K., Isaacs, I., & Allsop, A. (2010). "The relationship between transformation leadership behaviours, psychological and training outcomes in elite military recruits". *The Leadership Quarterly, Volume 21, (1),* 20-32.

House, R, J. (1977). *A 1977 theory of charismatic leadership. Leadership: The cutting edge.* Carbondale: Southern Illinois University Press.

House, R, J. (1999). Weber and neo-charismatic leadership paradigm: A response to Beyer. *The Leadership Quaterly, 10,* 563 – 574.

House, R, J. (1996). Path-goal theory of leadership: Lessons, legacy, and a reformulated theory. *The Leadership Quarterly, 7,* 323–352.

House, R, J., & Shamir, B. (1993). *Toward the integration of transformational, charismatic, and visionary theories.* San Diego, CA: Academic Press.

Howell, J, M., & Frost, P, J. (1989). A laboratory study of charismatic leadership. *Organizational Behaviour and Human Decision Processes, 43,* 243−269.

Jowett, S., & Chaundy, V. (2004). An investigation into the impact of coach leadership and coach athlete relationship on group cohesion. *Group Dynamics: Theory, Research and Practice, 8,* 302-311.

Jung, D., & Avolio, B. (2000). Opening the black box: An

experimental investigation of the mediating effects of trust and value congruence on transformational and transactional leadership. *Journal of Organizational Behaviour*, 21: 949-964.

Kirkpatrick, D.L., & Kirkpatrick, J.D. (1994). *Evaluating Training Programs*, Berrett-Koehler Publishers

Kram, K, E. (1985). *Mentoring at work*. Glenview, IL: Scott, Foresman and Company.

Maurer, T, J., & Tarulli, B, A. (1994). Investigation of perceived environment, perceived outcome, and person variables in relationship to voluntary development activity by employees. *Journal of Applied Psychology, 79*, 3–14.

McDermott, M., Levenson, A., & Newton, S. (2007). What coaching can and cannot do for your organization. *Human Resource Planning, 30*, 30–37.

Messmer, M. (2003). Building an effective mentoring program. *Strategic Finance, 84(8)*, 17–18.

Noe, R, A., & Schmitt, N. (1986). The influence of trainee attitudes on training effectiveness: test of a model. *Personnel Psychology, 39*, 497–523.

Patrick, J. (2006). *Effectiveness of Coaching Techniques in Military Training: Final Report,* Farnborough, QinetiQ Ltd.

Patrick, J., Ahmed, A., Hodgetts, H., Hutchings, P., Morgan, P., Scrase, G., Tombs, M and Watts, H. (2006). *Effectiveness of coaching techniques in military training*. Final Report HC-05-01-01-001 dated 7 Dec 06.

Podsakoff, P. M., MacKenzie, S. B., Moorman, R. H., & Fetter, R. (1990). Transformational leader behaviours and their effects on followers trust in leader, satisfaction, organizational citizenship behaviours. *Leadership Quarterly, 1*, 107-142.

Quiñones, M. A. (1995). Pre-training context effects: training assignment as feedback. *Journal of Applied Psychology, 80 (2)*, 226–238.

Reiss, K. (2007). *Leadership and coaching for educators.* Thousand Oaks, CA: Corwin Press.

Rokeach, M. (1973). *The Nature of human Values.* New York: Free Press.

Scandura, T, A., & Schriesheim, C, A. (1994). Leader–member exchange and supervisor career mentoring as complementary constructs in leadership research. *Academy of Management Journal, 37*, 1588–1602.

Schwartz, S, H. (1992). Universals in the content and structure of values: Theoretical advances and empirical tests in 20 countries. *Advances in Experimental Social Psychology, 25*, 1-65.

Shamir, B., & Howell, J, M. (1999). Organizational and contextual influences on the emergence and effectiveness of charismatic leadership. *The Leadership Quarterly, 10*, 257-283.

Sosik, J, J., Godshalk, V, M., & Yammarino, F, J. (2004). Transformational leadership, learning goal orientation, and expectations for career success in mentor-protégé relationships: A multiple levels of analysis perspective. *The leadership Quarterly 15*, 241-261.

Sosik, J, J., Avolio. B, J., & Kahai, S, S. (1997). Effects of leadership style and anonymity on group potency and effectiveness in a group decision support system environment. *Journal of Applied Psychology, 82*: 89-103.

Thorndike, Edward (1932), *The Fundamentals of Learning*, AMS Press Inc.

Van Hoose, D. (1999). Army civilian leadership training — past, present and future. *Military Review, 79 (3)*, 42–47.

Whitmore, J. (2003). *Coaching for Performance*. Nicholas Brealey Publishing.

M A. Grant

Suggested Code of Practice

The coach/mentor will acknowledge the dignity of all humanity. They will conduct themselves in a way which respects diversity and promotes equal opportunities.

It is the primary responsibility of the coach/mentor to provide the best possible service to the client and to act in such a way as to cause no harm to any client or sponsor.

The coach/mentor is committed to functioning from a position of dignity, autonomy and personal responsibility.

Competence

The coach/mentor will:

Ensure that their level of experience and knowledge is

sufficient to meet the needs of the client.

Ensure that their capability is sufficient to enable them to operate according to this Code of Ethics and any standards that may subsequently be produced.

Develop and then enhance their level of competence by participating in relevant training and appropriate Continuing Professional Development activities.

Maintain a relationship with a suitably-qualified supervisor, who will regularly assess their competence and support their development. The supervisor will be bound by the requirements of confidentiality referred to in this Code.

Context

The coach/mentor will:

Understand and ensure that the coach/mentoring relationship reflects the context within which the coach/mentoring is taking place.

Ensure that the expectations of the client and the sponsor are understood and that they themselves understand how those expectations are to be met.

Seek to create an environment in which client, coach/mentor and sponsor are focused on and have the opportunity for learning.

Boundary Management

The coach/mentor will:

At all times operate within the limits of their own

competence, recognise where that competence has the potential to be exceeded and where necessary refer the client either to a more experienced coach/mentor, or support the client in seeking the help of another professional, such as a counsellor, psychotherapist or business/financial advisor.

Be aware of the potential for conflicts of interest of either a commercial or emotional nature to arise through the coach/mentoring relationship and deal with them quickly and effectively to ensure there is no detriment to the client or sponsor.

Integrity

The coach/mentor will:

Maintain throughout the level of confidentiality which is appropriate and is agreed at the start of the relationship.

Disclose information only where explicitly agreed with the client and sponsor (where one exists), unless the coach/mentor believes that there is convincing evidence of serious danger to the client or others if the information is withheld.

Act within applicable law and not encourage, assist or collude with others engaged in conduct which is dishonest, unlawful, unprofessional or discriminatory.

Professionalism

The coach/mentor will:

Respond to the client's learning and development needs as

defined by the agenda brought to the coach/mentoring relationship.

Not exploit the client in any manner, including, but not limited to, financial, sexual or those matters within the professional relationship. The coach/mentor will ensure that the duration of the coach/mentoring contract is only as long as is necessary for the client/sponsor.

Understand that professional responsibilities continue beyond the termination of any coach/mentoring relationship. These include the following:

Maintenance of agreed confidentiality of all information relating to clients and sponsors.

Avoidance of any exploitation of the former relationship

Provision of any follow-up which has been agreed

Safe and secure maintenance of all related records and data

Demonstrate respect for the variety of different approaches to coaching and mentoring and other individuals in the profession.

Never represent the work and views of others as their own.

Ensure that any claim of professional competence, qualifications or accreditation is clearly and accurately explained to potential clients and that no false or misleading claims are made or implied in any published material.

Summary

The remainder of this book will focus on the technical and practical application of coaching, within gleaming performance results. If this is a career choice, then I recommend further exploration into the ethics, codes and business acumen associated with coaching.

Abbreviations

APEL – Approved Prior Education Learning.

ASLS – ARTD Staff Leadership School.

BD – Business Development.

CEO – Chief Executive Officer.

C&G – City & Guilds.

COO – Chief Operating Officer.

COE – Contemporary Operating Environment.

DCTS – Defence Centre of Training Support.

DIFD – Department for International Development.

DTLI – Differential Transformational Leadership Inventory.

DTTT – Defence Train the Trainer.

EQ – Emotional Quotient.

EMCC – European Mentoring & Coaching Council.

GROW – Goal, Reality, Options and Will.

HCDC - House of Commons Defence Committee.

HR – Human Resources.

ILM – Institute for Leadership and Management.

IQ – Intelligence Quotient.

KPA – Key Performance Area

KPIs – Key Performance Indicators.

MC – Master Coach.

ROI – Return On Investment.

SME – Subject Matter Expert.

STD - Self Determination Theory.

SUC – Sub Unit Coach.

TLB – Transformational Leadership Behaviour.

TO – Training Officer.

TTT – Train the Trainer.

VBL – Values Based Leadership.

UAE – United Arab Emirates.

UK – United Kingdom.

ABOUT THE AUTHOR

M A. Grant is a dedicated and motivated values driven individual, he has mentored leaders and supported organizations as they shape and develop their leadership styles and cultural identities.

He has more than twenty years strategic, advisory and operational experience in the fields of leadership, management and corporate innovation. This has stretched across a wide range of international governmental and private sector organizations.

He has a genuine interest in personnel development and the growth of human capital with a proven ability to unleash people's real potential.

.